HYPNOSIS

CONTROLLING THE INNER YOU

HANS HOLZER, PhD

SQUAREONE
PUBLISHERS

A word about gender: To avoid long and awkward phrases within sentences, the publisher has chosen to alternate the use of male and female pronouns according to chapter. Therefore, when referring to individuals in odd numbered chapters we use male pronouns, while even numbered chapters employ female pronouns.

Cover Designer: Jeannie Tudor
Editor: Kent Sturgis
Typesetter: Gary A. Rosenberg

Square One Publishers
115 Herricks Road
Garden City Park, NY 11040
(877) 900-BOOK
www.squareonepublishers.com

Library of Congress Cataloging-in-Publication Data

Holzer, Hans, 1920–
    Hypnosis : controlling the inner you / Hans Holzer.
        p. cm.
    Includes index.
    ISBN-13: 978-0-7570-0271-7 (pbk.)
    ISBN-10: 0-7570-0271-4 (pbk.)
    1. Hypnotism. I. Title.

BF1141.H748 2006
154.7—dc22

                                        200602631

Printed in the United States of America

10   9   8   7   6   5   4   3   2   1

Contents

Introduction

If you walk into a bookstore looking for information about hypnosis, the categories in which you find each book will give you a clue as to its author's take on this complex, sometimes controversial, and often misunderstood subject. Some titles are found with dense medical volumes. Others are found in psychology sections. Still others are found among books about the occult.

Books written by doctors and academics tend to be couched in technical terms. They generally include clinical case histories and are aimed at medical practitioners. These may put the average reader to sleep—no pun intended.

At the other end of the spectrum are books written by magicians and performers who regard hypnosis as entertainment. They dwell on special effects, hypnotic tricks, and proof that hypnosis really "works." Some books reveal techniques for do-it-yourself hypnosis, which can be risky if you do not know what you are doing.

Finally, you will find books written by parapsychologists, psychologists, hypnotists, and professional science writers who attempt to deal with the subject as a whole and from all points of view. Their purpose is to explain the use of hypnosis in modern society and to inform the public of the risks and rewards of hypnosis while providing a comprehensive handbook for readers seeking to use hypnosis to better their lives.

My book falls somewhat into the last category, but with some differences.

In *Hypnosis,* you will learn the fascinating history behind hypnosis while exploring what hypnosis is and the techniques that are used by professional hypnotists. I have created a factual yet interesting context for your understanding and, perhaps, appreciation of hypnosis. No such explanation is complete without exploring the wonders of sleep, so we will begin with this subject and the relationship between the conscious and the unconscious. You will learn, too, about how and why modern hypnosis helps treat problems related to sex, love, and relationships. Through other case studies, you will see that when hypnosis "suggests" that an ailing mind or body heal itself, the subject often responds by beginning the path towards wellness. Finally, we will visit the paranormal, and what hypnosis can potentially teach us about this field of study.

I wrote this book for two reasons.

First, I want to correct and clarify inaccuracies, distortion, and misconceptions. I want you to understand what hypnosis can, and cannot, do.

Second, I want to share my own experience and knowledge of the uses of hypnosis in research of parapsychology. My work encompasses extrasensory perception (ESP) and reincarnation, while also exploring a variety of other psychic phenomena that some might consider unorthodox but help create a more complete understanding of hypnosis.

On occasion, I have practiced psychotherapy as well, with some success. I believe that only when we consider the human personality as a whole and recognize hypnosis as an important element of the integrated mind-body-spirit, can we understand the usefulness, the effectiveness, and the power of hypnosis.

1

Hypnosis Through the Ages

Hypnosis has been practiced by medical professionals for more than two hundred years, but has had an "image" problem because of its historic roots in the occult.

A MIRACLE FROM THE GODS

Although hypnosis has been practiced since the beginning of time, the term "hypnosis" is relatively modern. Practitioners included the local shaman, medicine man, tribal priest, and, more recently, the medical doctor. In early societies, the phenomenon of hypnotic sleep or trance sleep was considered a miracle from the gods.

The word "hypnosis" is derived from *Hypnos*, the Greek god of sleep, brother of *Thanatos*, the god of death. The Greeks believed the world of the dead and the world of sleep were interrelated.

Explaining the Unknown

In the Stone Age, only a shaman could interpret communication with the gods, explain seemingly supernatural occurrences, and possess special knowledge.

One of the shaman's abilities was to ease pain by putting people to sleep. A common way to induce a hypnotic state was with chants, the rhythmical repetition of certain syllables or vowels by one or more voices for a period of time. Chanting a person to sleep put the conscious mind to rest, and allowed the shaman to gain entrance to one's unconscious.

Feeling No Pain

This "magic sleep" awed his followers. The subject of the shaman's spell was deeply asleep, yet did not feel pain when a wound was attended to! The "patient" was able to answer questions without awakening. Because primitive tribes had no knowledge of the nature of sleep or hypnosis as we know it today, it was believed that such techniques were a form of divine intercession. The shaman was respected, although often also feared.

SLEEP TRANCE

As the Stone Age society yielded first to the Bronze Age and then to the Iron Age, the technique of putting people into a temporary sleep trance became more sophisticated. The Egyptians and the Chinese worked independently of each other but came up with similar techniques. Both societies built "sleep temples" in which to conduct hypnosis. They experimented with herbs, special potions, and aromatics, to both open doors to the unconscious mind and reduce the risk that a subject would awaken suddenly during a medical treatment.

Understanding in Egypt

In ancient Egypt, the priest and physician were familiar with the techniques of putting people to sleep in order to relieve their pain, heal their wounds, or extract information from them. Special prayers were used to lull a person to a state of drowsiness, which would be followed by a deep sleep. Everything in the arsenal of the modern hypnotist was used, from drugs to sound effects to verbal manipulation of the conscious mind. The only difference between the Egyptian practitioner and his modern counterpart is the Egyptian's presumption that deities and supernatural powers made the process of hypnosis possible.

Fearing the Evil Eye

Many people during the Middle Ages, particularly those in southern Europe, feared a negative form of hypnosis known as the "evil eye." It was believed that a mere look from one person's eyes into another's could bring on a hypnotic state coupled with a loss of will power. It was thought that the effects could be counteracted by certain hand gestures. To this day, the superstition of the evil eye is strong among some peasants in parts of Spain, southern Italy, and Latin America. I will tell you more about the evil eye in Chapter 9. For now, suffice it to say that the supernatural connotations related to the evil eye are quite simply erroneous.

MEDICAL TREATMENT

Born in 1734, Swiss physician Friedrich Anton Mesmer is considered by some to be the father of hypnotism. Mesmer demonstrated his unusual powers to select groups of French and Swiss high society. He appeared wearing a flowing gown and carrying an iron rod. He believed that a form of electrical power, an "animal magnetism," came from some outer world through his body. From his body, this force reached his patients through the iron rod with which he touched them, resulting in cures for the ill as well as many strange reactions in his subjects. Although many of the cures he was believed to have affected are today understood to have been spontaneous remission, the strange behaviors were a result of a hypnotic power Mesmer possessed that was unknown even to him. Although he never fully understood the power he discovered, it was known as *Mesmerism* for the next hundred years.

The word "mesmerize," meaning to spellbind or hypnotize, is derived from the name Mesmer.

Denouncing Hypnosis

During the nineteenth century, the Scottish physician Dr. James Braid became the first scientifically trained professional to use hypnosis in his treatments. In 1841, he witnessed the act of a Swiss magnetizer and began conducting experiments at his clinic to find a scientific explanation for the performance. Because he believed there was a connection between the process and sleep, Dr. Braid coined the term "hypnotism," derived from *Hypnos,* the Greek god of sleep.

A decade or so later, the French physician Jean-Martin Charcot, the German physician Hippolyte Bernheim, and the American physician Alva Curtis began to utilize newly discovered hypnotic techniques. For a time, hypnosis was fashionable. During and after the scientific awakening following World War I, however, many medical practitioners denounced it as the work of quacks and occultists. (See "Fear of the Unknown," below.)

Then, following World War II, the medical profession gradually came to recognize the importance and potential of hypnosis in their treatments. Dentists began to use hypnosis to relieve pain. Qualified physicians, too, who wish to use hypnosis in their practices routinely seek out training in its techniques—although some physicians from older generations will have nothing to do with it. This resistance may be due in part to their distaste for stage hyp-

Fear of the Unknown

In the 1950s, my career had just begun, and hypnotism scared people. This was before it became better understood and more widely accepted. The idea of demonstrating it or experimenting with it was unthinkable, particularly to those in authority. The belief persisted among television executives, for example, that masses of TV viewers might fall under hypnotic spells merely by watching a competent hypnotist perform on the air.

Academia was no more enlightened. At the New York Institute of Technology, where I taught, I was told not to conduct hypnosis experiments or demonstrations in the classroom. The institute's legal staff feared that hypnosis might hurt someone, or that someone would claim to be hurt. It was thought this could be costly to the university, not to mention a source of embarrassment.

The truth about hypnosis is that it is neither mysterious nor dangerous when conducted properly.

nosis, although the number of such practitioners has radically declined due to competition from another form of entertainment—television.

CONCLUSION

As far back as the Stone Age, primitive forms of hypnosis were practiced as part magic, part interpretation of the supernatural, and part healing. Its widespread acceptance has only been within the last century, and it is now used as a tool in modern medicine. Yet, in some ways, it retains a connection to its ancient roots.

2

The Wonders of Sleep

Sleep and dreams are closely related to hypnosis, when a subject is lulled into trance-like sleep. What is happening in our mind when we sleep and dream?

PERSONALITY AND SLEEP

To understand hypnosis and its potential, you must first understand the human personality and recognize that sleep is more than simply a period of rest and withdrawal from physical activity.

Sleep and dreams have always been connected. One without the other is unthinkable. William Shakespeare wrote of Hamlet's desire to "sleep, perchance to dream." The hope is expressed that while asleep one may have a revelation in a dream. Sleep is the other half of our consciousness, as we are either awake or asleep. Both halves are equally important to life. Many things happen in the sleep state besides the restoration of energies or reception of dreams.

Disconnecting Conscious Mind

There is a vital difference between the waking state and the sleep state. When we are awake, the conscious part of our mind dominates, and our experiences are evaluated on the surface of our rational thinking. When we are asleep, on the other hand, our conscious is temporarily disconnected, and our unconscious takes over.

Our conscious and unconscious are also fundamentally different. While the conscious connects closely with all logical thinking processes, the unconscious is unable to think logically. The unconscious is the channel through which all psychic experiences, feelings, and emotions flow. Without it, we would be mere intelligent animals. With it, we are emotional creatures capable of great genius. The completeness of our personalities depends on interplay between the conscious and unconscious sides of our minds. When there is disturbance between them, ill health results.

What we do while awake is known. What we do while we are asleep is not. Obviously, there is a restoration of physical energy during the sleep state. Mental energy is replenished, too, although this is not to say that mental activity ceases when you are asleep. The opposite is true. Freed from the shackles of the logical conscious mind, the unconscious is given free rein to express itself and to roam at will beyond the boundaries of time and space. This can be turned into the creative efforts of writers, artists, and inventors. During sleep, we may have contact with a reservoir of information variously called the "world mind," the "universal consciousness," and the "world beyond."

Most psychic experiences take place during the sleep state. It is easier to establish contact between the nonphysical and physical realms when the conscious mind is temporarily excluded. In sleep, the unconscious mind is in full control and has no boundaries.

THE DREAM STATE

Sleep supports the "dream state." Dreams are to sleep what thoughts and actions are to being awake. Just as being awake does not necessarily mean that one is always thinking or acting, being asleep does not mean that one is always dreaming. But most of the time when we are asleep, we dream; and just as logical thinking and deliberate action are impossible without being awake, dreams are impossible except in the sleep state. There are two rare exceptions: sleepwalking and visions experienced during an awakened state. I'll discuss these phenomena in more detail later.

Sleeping and Dreaming

Sleep and dreams are connected with hypnosis. In sleep, the body functions slow down. The vital activities of the body are reduced to such a low level that all remaining energies are freed for regeneration and storing of mental information, with only a small portion of the energy directed toward routine maintenance of the body. Nature has seen to it that this occurs regularly by having natural weariness of body and mind necessitate sleep.

Despite the frequent poetic allusion to sleep resembling death, the two have nothing in common except perhaps the superficial appearance of a reclining and immobile person with eyes closed and no outward signs of life.

MIND AND SPIRIT ASLEEP

If we recognize the trinity of body, mind, and spirit—that which religion calls the "soul"—then the question arises as to what happens to the mind and spirit when the body is asleep. The mind continues to function. Without its function, the control centers of the brain could not be activated and the body would cease to stay alive for even a fraction of a second. Yet the mind, as we have learned, consists of several levels, the most important of which are conscious and unconscious levels.

During sleep, the conscious mind is inactive while the unconscious takes over. Although the unconscious is without critical abilities, it regulates vital functions of the body at low levels during the sleep period. The conscious mind is given this time to recharge from the life force within the body. As far as the spirit is concerned, it can either be put to rest or remain active during sleeping hours. This is not so much the choice of the person as it is a matter of conditions.

When the person has no unresolved residue from daytime activities, and sleep is a routine function, little psychic material will enter into the unconscious while she is asleep. But how many of us have no hang-ups, no leftover issues, and no unresolved problems?

Taking Unresolved Issues to Bed

Unfortunately, most people do not come to terms with all of their problems during their daily waking hours. Some of these unresolved issues carry over into their sleep state. When this happens, the unconscious mind goes to work. It replays these unresolved problems and suggests solutions, in this way functioning semi-independently. It is then, too, that *extrasensory perception* (ESP)—the ability of certain people to become aware of things by use of a perceptive sense beyond the five normal human senses—enters the unconscious and is either sorted out for remembrance upon awakening or sent deeper down to the symbolic inner layers of consciousness that only a psychoanalyst or hypnotist can probe for clarification.

The duration and depth of sleep range from light and short to long and deep, depending on the needs of the individual person. There are no standard sleeping periods. What may be too little for one person is too much for another. The old standard rule that we need eight hours of sleep daily applies to a fraction of the population. It is, however, known that long periods of sleeplessness will lead to degeneration of all faculties, both physical and mental.

PROBLEMS OF INSOMNIA

Insomnia is a major problem in today's world. Coupled with it are occasional incidents of sleepwalking, known in more technical language as *somnambulism*. Causes of insomnia can often be found in the deeper levels of consciousness, and are often related to unresolved problems that are ignored or not understood.

Many insomniacs may be unable to sleep because they feel the need to apply themselves to an important problem. In this respect, insomnia mimics the urgency of guilt, although it is not nearly as strongly expressed or as easily understood. The more the insomniac tries to will herself to sleep, the less likely she is to succeed. Similarly to hypnosis and suggestion, the more the command is forced on a person, the more resistance is aroused, and the command will not be executed.

Inducing sleep through sedatives is only partially successful. They may put the body to sleep, but cannot reach to ease the mind or the spirit. Sedatives should be used only in emergencies and in extreme cases where sleep is vitally important to recovery from illness or injury. Usually insomnia is caused by unresolved material in the unconscious mind, and only suggestion or hypnosis will bring more permanent results. If physical means are preferred, then only natural herbal remedies should be used that do not drug but instead gently relax the body, thus incidentally inducing sleep.

Inhibiting Sleep

We all differ in our tolerance of conditions that inhibit sleep. The average person's sleep is rarely inhibited, for example, if a bedroom is too cold, warm, dry, or damp. Yet there are those of us who cannot sleep if a room is not perfectly balanced in temperature and humidity. In particular, an excessively humid bedroom is likely to awaken such a sleeper. Improper posture can also cut sleep short. The schools of thought on proper sleeping position run the gamut from lying totally horizontal on a hard surface with a hard pillow to being propped up with two pillows in order to facilitate breathing. The majority of people, however, will find one pillow and a moderately resistant sleeping surface best suited to their sleep needs.

Sleeping "With the Tide"

We are still learning about earth radiation and how it affects sleep and consciousness. In Germany, this has been studied intensively for many years. Experiments suggest that the position of the bed in relation to the axis of the earth directly affects the nature and quality of sleep. If you have trouble sleeping, therefore, you might change the orientation of your bed. I believe that the rotation of the earth on its axis and the magnetic field this creates has a direct connect with each human being's magnetic field—and, thus, also has an effect on the sleep state. Think of this as swimming against the tide. If you determine which way the tide is going, and turn in that direction, you will be carried along, whereas trying to go in the opposite direction will cause you to encounter great difficulty.

SLEEPWALKING

In sleepwalking, the dramatic fantasy becomes so strong that it is able to overcome the inertia of the body in the sleeping condition and manipulate it into quasi-wakefulness. The sleepwalker will

Rare Case of Sleepwalker Having Sex

New Scientist magazine reported in October 2004 that sleep medicine experts had successfully treated a rare case of a woman having sex with strangers while sleepwalking.

The middle-aged sleepwalker would be sleeping in the middle of the night when she would leave her house and have sexual intercourse with strangers. This occurred for several months, but the woman retained no memory of these events. Although evidence such as mysterious condoms appearing around the house suggested a problem, it wasn't until the woman's partner woke during the night to discover her gone and searched the neighborhood for her that the root of the problem was discovered. It was at that time that he saw her involved in sexual activities.

"Incredulity is the leading player in cases like this," says Peter Buchanan, the doctor in charge of the case. Buchanan is a sleep physician at Sydney's Woolcock Institute of Medical Research in Sydney. He became convinced that the case was a real sleepwalking phenomenon rather than a hoax after studying a combination of factors including the couple's distress and an in-depth clinical evaluation.

climb up and down stairs, open doors, and even walk out onto a roof without falling. (See "Sleepwalking 'Runs' in the Family," page 16.) For the most part, the sleepwalker exercises amazing judgment, though not consciously. The sleepwalker is guided by the unconscious mind. Touching or awakening such a person may be dangerous. Many sleepwalkers have been found to be in a psychic trance. This trance differs to one brought on with the help of a medium because it is involuntary, while one caused by a medium is controlled.

Sleep occupies a somewhat mysterious place in human beliefs and religion. Nearly all civilizations regard sleep as an opening to the other world. It is during sleep that one can visit the dead and the dead can visit her. In ancient Greece, the gods came down from Mount Olympus to appear to mortals during sleep. Christians believe that friendly saints visit their petitioners during sleep. The Old Testament speaks of a number of instances in which God visited and gave instructions to the patriarchs while they slept. Adam, for example, was asleep when spoken to by God.

To murder a man in his sleep is considered grossly immoral, and has been considered such by even the most primitive societies. "Macbeth doth murder sleep, the innocent sleep, that nourishes life," Macbeth heard after his first crime, and this thought reflects universal thinking that predates Shakespeare.

In 1992, the Canadian Supreme Court upheld the acquittal of Kenneth Parks, who said he was sleepwalking when he drove fourteen miles, stabbed his mother-in-law to death and seriously injured his father-in-law.

—CNN News

EMOTIONAL RESTORATION

Healing takes place during sleep. This includes not only physical healing, but also less tangible inner healing. This emotional restoration is made possible by a force from within that is not completely understood.

It may not be surprising that sexual intercourse most naturally takes place during sleeping hours. Because sex is an emotionally tinged activity, it has more impact when the unconscious mind is in charge, which occurs when the couple is not quite awake. The more a couple is able to cut themselves loose from logic and conscious thinking, the more they will enjoy sexual intercourse.

Lest we assume sleep is a special gift to humans, it is important to understand that animals sleep just as we do, even if their minds have not developed to our levels of consciousness. Even plants—in fact, all kinds of living matter—go through periods of rest and withdrawal. Seen broadly and in a universal perspective, the regular interplay of waking and sleeping represents in part the vibrations of life. Highs followed by lows in a continuous cycle represent the positive and negative factors in life. This brings us back to the ultimate and simple equation that all life exists because a positive element is brought together with a negative element, interacts with it, and repeats itself.

Sleepwalking "Runs" in the Family

When we moved into our first house, a two-story, I realized that my son was a sleepwalker. Good timing, right? I was at work one night and got a phone call from my boyfriend, who was a little angry. He was ranting about how my son had gotten up, walked down the stairs past the bathroom, and come into the kitchen. There, he pulled down his pants and peed in the dog's water bowl! My boyfriend thought my son had done this on purpose.

I pointed out that sleepwalking runs in my family and that apparently the little guy has picked up the family trait. The males in the family seem to start right after they are potty-trained. My son was three. The sleepwalking starts with them attempting to get to the restroom. Unfortunately, the boys tend to miss the bathroom altogether and end up whizzing in boots, trashcans, hallways, and now dog bowls.

It could've been worse! An uncle once peed in his own boot while sleepwalking. This was an unpleasant surprise for him when he put on his boots the next morning.

—posted anonymously on www.talkaboutsleep.com, August 2005

Most of us have several hundred dream segments in a single night, although many are not remembered later. The dreams, as we remember them, are both short and long. Yet this is an illusion, because there can be no true understanding of duration when dealing with dreams.

Researching Dreams

The late Professor Hornell Hart of Duke University tested some three hundred students to learn about their dreams. Awakening them at frequent intervals, he insisted that his subjects write down all of their dreams. He discovered that the dreams came by the hundreds, that a certain percentage of them were of paranormal origin with content going beyond the laws of science, and that the dreams would not have been remembered had not the students been awakened.

Dr. Stanley Krippner of Maimonides Hospital in Brooklyn, New York also studied dreams. His focus was on the different levels of dream-sleep. He found that *rapid eye movement* (REM)—a sleep stage during which the eyes flutter and the neurons act similarly to how they act when the subject is awake—is an index to the depth and nature of each dream experience.

FOUR KINDS OF DREAMS

People dream about many different things. All dreams, however, can be put into one of the following four categories.

Unpleasant Dreams

We often call unpleasant dreams "nightmares." They are usually full of fear and anxiety, and they often lack logic. Threats, fears, monsters, and impossible situations are common fodder for unpleasant dreams. These fantasies can be caused by sickness or physical discomfort; overindulgence in food, alcohol, or drugs; or rapid withdrawal from drugs. Sometimes these dreams occur because of traumatic events in the dreamer's life. Yet, they often occur with no special significance and often may be able to be relieved with the usual remedies for an upset stomach.

Symbolic Dreams

Symbolic dreams are basic fodder for the psychoanalyst. They contain fragments and suppressed material from the dreamer's past, present, and occasionally even an anticipated future, as well as symbolic representations of desires, objects, and other elements in her life that cannot be discussed openly while she is awake.

Many people agree that dreams represent much valuable material regarding the inner workings of a person's mind, and contain keys to a person's real desires and objectives. There is much truth to this. Skilled analysts can bring these suppressed emotions and desires to the surface so they can be discussed and the negative factors potentially eliminated. Psychoanalysts from the Jungian school generally like patients to analyze and comment on this material themselves, after which they add their own interpretations. The subject's own analysis can be as insightful as the actual dream.

Let's look at an example of a symbolic dream. A man dreamt of his dead father suddenly returning to life and moving in with him. He finds himself in a quandary regarding his wife's feelings about this invasion, yet he is unable to ask his dead father to leave. This hints at some sort of guilt complex toward the father—something the man failed to do while his father was still alive, perhaps because of conflicts between his duties toward his father and his duties toward his wife. Symbolism is easily recognizable because it uses plausible and possible situations, although the events have not actually occurred and most likely will not.

"True" Dreams

True dreams are rare, occurring in people with above-average gifts of ESP. The dreamer receives detailed, precise information about either past events unknown to the dreamer or future events. The material is received as if it was dictated by an outside source and is usually remembered fully on awakening. In fact, true dreams are often remembered with such clarity that the dreamer cannot quickly shake the memory. Sometimes, the message from the dream may be received again or even several times. A true dream is rarely frightening unless it warns of a future disaster.

A large percentage of psychic experiences take place in true dreams. The connection to the unconscious is easier than in other kinds of dreams. All precognitive dreams, prophetic visions, and ESP "hunches" are similar in nature. The material does not seem to

---

Share Your Nightmares

The International Study for the Association of Dreams offers a twenty-four-hour, toll-free hotline (866-DRMS-911) for adults and children who experience dreams with strong overtones of fear, devastation, overwhelming shame, guilt, humiliation, or mutilation, as well as dreams of falling, burning, and other upsetting events. Telephone volunteers do not offer counseling but can provide information on available resources for those wanting to know more about why they have nightmares or who wish to seek professional counseling.

originate within the sleeper. Instead, it appears to come from an outside source, with the sleeper acting as channel.

However, opinions differ about this. Some feel that the ESP of the sleeper produces the paranormal phenomenon. Others accept the existence of another dimension in which material unknown to the sleeper exists independently and is channeled through her unconscious mind to reach her conscious mind on waking. I am convinced of the latter. Frequently, a spiritual entity seems to be the source. Not every precognitive dream can be attributed to ESP. There remains a large residue of dream material not explainable without belief in continuance of life beyond the physical state.

The Out-of-Body Experience

The "out-of-body" experience is referred to as *astral projection.* In this process, a sleeper is propelled from her physical body and travels through a different plane of existence, sometimes at great speed and for great distances. She remains fully conscious of her journey. These experiences vary. In the simplest form, the sleeper merely rises from her physical shell and observes her own sleeping body below. She may find herself gliding through the walls and outward over the landscape. In most recorded instances, the dreamer sees nothing unusual—that is, nothing she would not see if traveling in her physical body.

Occasionally, sleepers have reported beautiful landscapes and unworldly conditions as an astral projection. Dreamers who have received anesthetics during surgery, in particular, tend to report this experience. Without a doubt, some of the hallucinations in these cases can be attributed to the anesthetic.

Consider the case of "Mrs. Y" of New York City. Her out-of-body experience has been authenticated. She found herself unexpectedly "flying"—without benefit of an airplane—across the country to her sister's home in California. Once there, she noticed that certain structural changes had been made to the house since her previous visit. Her sister stood on the lawn, wearing a green dress. A moment later, she was back in her bed in New York. On awakening, she wrote down details of what she assumed was an unusual dream. Then, she wrote her sister in California and includ-

Investigating Astral Projection

Years ago, during experimental sessions at the New York headquarters of the Cayce Foundation, there was a case of an induced out-of-body experience. Two teams of researchers were positioned in two apartments twenty blocks apart. One team opened a book to a certain page on a table and placed a particular flower in a vase. In the other apartment, a young man named Stanley was artificially put under—that is, it was suggested under hypnosis that he journey forth in an astral projection and visit the other apartment.

During the next half hour, while Stanley "slept," none of the observers in the first apartment saw him, and those in the second apartment noted that his body did not seem to become unusually agitated while he was under. Yet when Stanley woke up, he proceeded to accurately describe the first apartment, including the book's title, the page to which the book was left open, and the flower's color and location. He remembered floating through the apartments and seeing himself. He also recalled an unnatural bluish-white light.

Out-of-body experiences are not uncommon. They occur most often among people who receive messages from other worlds and people who have unusually loose bonds between their conscious and unconscious minds.

There is no known danger in astral projection, despite the dire warnings of the late Madame Blavatsky, who warned that evil entities could enter the physical body of the astral traveler while she was traveling. I know of no such case.

ed the details of her dream. To her surprise and her sister's shock, she had indeed seen the house correctly. Work had been done on it—and her sister had purchased a new green dress just before the out-of-body "journey" took place.

Out-of-body travelers usually report a sensation of falling from great heights just prior to awakening. This feeling, often coupled with a sensation of dizziness or spinning, appears to be a counter-reaction to the stepping down of speed or vibrations when the spirit returns to the physical body. The reentry of the spirit into the denser physical body requires an adjustment of speed from very fast astral travel to the much slower movement of life in the body. Rather than falling, the traveler is merely slowing down rapidly.

These four kinds of dreams cover all experiences. Just about everyone has experience in more than one dream category, and it is not unusual to experience all four. Because the principle of hypnosis involves a loosening of the bonds between the conscious and unconscious mind, and because this also occurs during the dream state, a complete understanding of sleep and dreams is important to understanding hypnosis.

CONCLUSION

The variations of sleep and the different ways we dream are of great interest to professional hypnotists because hypnosis involves an induced sleep state. It is important, therefore, to understand the relationship between being asleep and being awake, and between the unconscious mind and the conscious mind, while also remaining aware of their fundamental differences. The sleep state and dreams are an integral part of the investigation of hypnosis.

3

What Exactly Is Hypnosis?

When hypnotized, the subject's conscious mind is put to rest, leaving the subject in a trance-like state in which he is highly susceptible to "suggestions" that the hypnotist can plant in his unconscious mind. Not everyone can be hypnotized, and complete trust between hypnotist and subject is crucial to the procedure. Successful hypnosis, however, can be useful for many reasons. In this chapter, we will take a closer look at the effects of hypnosis both during and after the process.

A MIND DIVIDED

Hypnosis is a state in which the mind does not function normally because the conscious and unconscious are no longer in balance. The subject surrenders his conscious mind to the hypnotist while the unconscious mind continues to function, as it must in order to sustain life in the physical body.

The term "hypnotism" is misleading, although it has become part of everyday language and is a term used widely. Any term ending in "-ism" suggests a human attitude, such as nationalism, communism, fatalism, and vegetarianism. Yet hypnotism is *not* an attitude. Rather, it is a state of consciousness.

Surrendering Freely

Hypnosis is a highly personal relationship between two people, the hypnotist and his subject. The hypnotist can influence the subject's conscious mind only to the extent that the subject will allow. This is important to understand. The temporary surrender of the mind during a hypnotic state is strictly voluntary, but this surrender must be complete and without doubt for hypnosis to successfully take place.

Whether or not the subject accepts the effectiveness of hypnosis prior to its occurrence has little bearing on the results. The subject's attitude toward the hypnotist, on the other hand, is important. Without complete trust, hypnosis will not take place or, at best, will have limited results. Because the hypnotist-subject relationship is so vital, and because success depends on factors beyond the mere technique, hypnosis works best with a single subject. The notion that people can simultaneously be put into a group hypnotic trance against their individual wishes is nonsense. Even the stage hypnotist, who uses a different approach towards hypnosis than either the physician or the researcher, cannot hypnotize more than one person at a time.

THE POWER OF SUGGESTION

Hypnosis is based on suggestion. The power of suggestion varies with each hypnotist and even more so with each subject's ability to accept suggestion.

In some people, the inclination to accept suggestions from a hypnotist exists because they do not mind being told what to do. Other people can easily be brought under hypnotic control simply because they have a personality like a vacuum that is quickly filled by a hypnotist's suggestions. Having said this, however, I should add that such people who easily accept suggestions do not necessarily make the best subjects for hypnosis.

Different Subjects

The best subjects are balanced people with one or more specific problems who voluntarily seek hypnotic suggestion to help them deal with these problems. Those most likely to fail include anyone emotionally disturbed or anyone who uses hypnosis as a crutch with which to hobble through the everyday realities of life. These people should not attempt hypnosis.

Hypnosis can improve your life. Certain ailments, mainly emotional, do not yield to conventional medicine and do not respond to traditional psychotherapy, analysis, or psychiatric treatment. On occasion, these cases can be dealt with successfully through in-depth hypnosis. I have experience with such cases. Medical doctors often suggest their patients see me when all else has failed.

Trust Is Important

Because hypnosis is so dependent on trust between hypnotist and subject, subjects are not likely to be open to suggestions from doubtful sources. Success is 90-percent willingness of the subject to be hypnotized and 10-percent skill of the hypnotist. I have never known any unethical hypnotists who overcame the resistance of subjects and hypnotized them into states that went against the subjects' moral, ethical, or emotional codes.

Comic-strip hypnosis, in which the master flicks a finger and the subject falls into a deep hypnotic sleep, also does not exist. A good working relationship between subject and hypnotist is best developed with frank discussion of problems at hand, a subject's understanding and acceptance of the process, identification of the subject's need for hypnosis, and other social and moral factors.

Despite the importance of suggestion, no skilled hypnotist would be needed if hypnosis was merely suggestion, and a subject was amenable to suggestions from other sources. The difference is that suggestion must be given to the unconscious mind on a level not usually available in ordinary social intercourse. The conversation preceding the session can give the professional hypnotist valuable clues regarding the subject's likely reactions.

HYPNOSIS AT WORK

Hypnosis can be put to good use as part of medical treatment for both physical and mental illnesses, as a remedy for personality adjustments and improvements, and as a tool in parapsychology and related research. Let's look at specific uses of hypnosis.

Hastening Psychoanalysis

Hypnosis can shorten the time required for psychoanalysis to a matter of weeks. Ordinarily, this process takes months. The success of hypnosis in this area depends on good rapport between the therapist and the patient and on a state of positive "transference." *Transference,* in the context of therapy, means the redirection of a patient's feelings toward the therapist.

Assisting Natural Childbirth

Hypnosis can be an invaluable aid during natural childbirth. The absence of drugs improves the newborn's health prospects, and the drug-free mother regains her strength more quickly than if she had been drugged.

Lessening Pain

Hypnosis can be used as a painkiller or pain deterrent. It works more effectively in short, simple treatments than it does in complicated treatments involving extended pain. For instance, hypnosis can be effective in the extraction of a tooth. The hypnotic approach is simply a suggestion that the pain impulse not be transmitted by the injury or sensitive area, in effect delaying and dissipating the pain.

Of course, hypnosis does not cure whatever ailment is the source of the pain, and this fact causes some physicians to question its usefulness. However, the suppression of pain does not mean that other treatment should be stopped. A patient free from pain is a better patient than one who is suffering.

"Adjusting" Personality

Many people are capable of more productive and happy lives if certain *inhibiting factors*—negative personality traits—are removed from their conscious minds. Under the suggestion of a skilled hypnotist, these inhibiting factors may be brought to the surface, analyzed, and effectively removed. In their place, more positive factors can be implanted in the unconscious mind through the power of suggestion.

The word "psyche" means different things to different people. In Greek, it means "self." In modern psychology, it refers to the mind or mental state. A religious synonym is "soul" or "spirit."

Modifying Behavior

Another practical application of hypnosis includes work with social maladjustments such as excessive smoking, drinking, and drug abuse; nervous reactions such as tics, stammering, and compulsive movements or speech; milder asocial behaviors such as promiscuity and kleptomania; and a wide range of psychoneurotic problems. Psychoanalysis using hypnosis can also deal with more complex problems ranging from severe psychoneurotic states to the psychotic. Keep in mind, however, that any hypnotic work with true psychotics or schizophrenics should not be performed unless the hypnotist is medically trained, and the treatment would best be done under institutional conditions.

A common misconception is that a subject replaces an old bad habit with a new bad habit once the first habit is removed through hypnosis. This is not so. When the hypnotist touches on some undesirable habit pattern, he does not merely remove it. Rather, he explores its basic causes and adjusts the positive factors as well as the undesirable habit. In addition, a counter-thought is injected into the subject's unconscious mind to make sure that the resulting vacuum is properly filled with a positive thought pattern.

Other Functions

Uses of hypnosis go well beyond standard treatments that address personal issues.

Investigating Parapsychology

Hypnosis is used in work involving aspects of parapsychology, particularly in cases where the researcher probes the unconscious mind for possible reincarnation memories. This is regression, a process by which a person is gradually led back in time through gradual stages until the moment of birth is reached. Ordinarily, that is where it ends. In parapsychological experiments, regression is taken beyond the threshold of birth to alleged former lives.

Dr. Ian Stevenson's classic work in this field, *Twenty Cases Suggestive of Reincarnation,* clearly points to the existence of previous-life memories in certain people. I, myself, have experimented in this area. The surprising results I have found provided me with enough fascinating material to publish the book, *Born Again.*

Achieving a Trance State

Hypnosis is used to induce the so-called *trance state,* in which the conscious bonds between body and personality are severed temporarily, so that a supposed foreign entity may take over the speech mechanism and other functions of the entranced person, who is called the *medium.* Often this is part of an investigation of a psychic event.

In the trance state, the medium—who is a psychic person—becomes another personality. Usually this is a supposedly deceased person, who communicates through the medium. The deceased person must prove his identity to the satisfaction of the researcher in such a way that there can be no doubt as to the authenticity of the phenomenon. This includes relating intimate and detailed knowledge of the deceased person's life—information that cannot be traced back to the medium or the researcher. Hypnosis is not necessary for a trance to take place, but it reduces the time it takes a medium to fall into trance.

Once that state has been reached, hypnosis is of no value and neither helps nor hinders the process. However, it becomes a valuable tool at the end of a trance investigation. After the medium has returned to his own consciousness, remnants of the personality and traumatic experiences of the deceased person may remain behind.

Suggestion is used to wipe out these remnants. The medium is taken into a deep state of hypnosis. Then a suggestion is implanted that all memories of another person be removed and that the medium return immediately to his own conscious self on awakening.

This is generally successful, and a medium thus treated does not retain any of the undesirable effects of having been in trance or having remnants of the supposedly deceased person linger in his own mind.

It should be emphasized that nothing alien can be induced in the subject that isn't acceptable to the unconscious mind. True, the skilled hypnotist may enhance a subject's innate skills or talents to the point where they become markedly improved or where a sense of security makes their application much easier. But the complete domination of a subject's mind by another is simply not possible. When unusual behavior results, it is not due to the hypnotist's injection of foreign thoughts into the unconscious mind but rather to the realization of thought and action patterns that the subject was not aware of while awake.

Many people harbor hostility, amoral thoughts, or asocial behavior patterns in their unconscious mind. Under normal conditions these impulses are suppressed. In hypnosis, the cover is ripped off the secret hiding places, and the suppressed patterns are brought to the forefront. First they are expressed and then they are eliminated through suggestion. This practice may embarrass the subject, but the continued harboring of suppressed undesirable behaviors is potentially far more damaging than a brief expression of unorthodox actions or ideas. No one need fear that he will act strangely under hypnosis unless there is within him some unexpressed desire that needs to be expressed. Because hypnosis typically takes place privately—as it should—no such behavior need cause lasting embarrassment.

RISK FACTORS

I know of no case in which extreme hostility such as murder or violence has resulted from hypnotic treatment. However, when we deal with psychotic subjects, there may be risk of awakening such sleeping impulses. That is why all hypnotic work with psychotics should be done with proper safeguards. Yet when working with ordinary people, including even psychoneurotics, there is no need to fear that criminal action may result from the use of hypnosis.

Hypnosis performed for entertainment, however, is less desirable. There are several ways in which it can be risky.

Inadequate Setup for and Removal of Suggestions

The time limits put on a stage performance reduce the preparation period, which is so vital to the process's success. Unskilled stage hypnotists also often forget to remove all post-hypnotic suggestions—that is, suggestions made during hypnosis to be acted on later. I'll tell you more about post-hypnotic suggestions shortly.

During performances, members of the audience other than those on stage do occasionally become partially or completely hypnotized as well, especially if they are sitting near the stage. This does not mean that entire audiences fall under the spell of the hypnotist, because essentially hypnosis is a one-on-one process. Occasionally, however, people may accidentally fall under its spell. Because stage hypnosis is rarely done with professional oversight and controls, anyone volunteering to become part of a performance may be asking for trouble.

Possibility of Injury

Stage hypnotists like to include physical phenomena into their acts. This may include *catalepsis,* a state of suggestion-induced rigidity in which the subject's body becomes so rigid that it can support great weights. Stage hypnotists may demonstrate this by having several people stand or sit on the stiff, extended body of a subject. There is the unfortunate possibility that the subject may come out of hypnosis suddenly and sustain injury. On the other hand, testing the insensitivity of the subject to pain with pins and needles can be entertaining and rarely results in injury. (The inset "For Fun and Profit" on page 31 further discusses stage hypnotists.)

Regardless, injury can occur if the hypnosis is not applied skillfully or if the subject's personal problems, quirks, weaknesses, and other traits are not sufficiently known to the hypnotist.

For Fun and Profit

In the hypnotism shows of Las Vegas, as well as the traveling hypnotism demonstrations on the college circuit, hypnotism is used primarily for entertainment purposes. It's an amazing experience watching somebody turn ordinary people, perhaps your friends or family, into outrageous performers. The power of suggestion and imagination, and the lowering of inhibition, does make for a fantastic show.

Yet, these demonstrations only scratch the surface of what hypnotism can do—all the suggestions are intentionally frivolous, to ensure that nobody gets hurt. The hypnotist uses his or her access to the unconscious mind only to play with the subject. More involved, one-on-one hypnotism uses this access to affect long-term changes in the subject.

—howstuffworks.com

Use of Mechanical Devices

I oppose use of mechanical devices such as lights, candles, sounds, and moving objects to induce hypnosis. Only hypnosis accomplished with purely verbal suggestions can promise no after effects whatsoever. A skilled hypnotist does not need mechanical gadgets when working with a good, skilled subject. No mechanical tool can create a good working relationship between hypnotist and subject if one does not exist.

Just as questionable, and potentially harmful, is using hypnosis as a parlor game or an idle experiment for mere curiosity's sake. Your knowing how to put someone under hypnosis does not guarantee your ability to bring the subject out safely and fully.

Involvement of Smoking, Heavy Drinking, and Drug Use

Smoking, heavy drinking, and drug use are incompatible with hypnosis. Nervous subjects who cannot bring themselves to relax sufficiently for hypnosis may have one or two glasses of wine, but under no circumstances should they take tranquilizers or other chemical agents. Hypnotists should make sure that their subjects have not taken any such substances for at least twenty-four hours prior to the hypnosis attempt.

CONCLUSION

Open and honest communication between the hypnotist and his subject—and the explicit trust that arises from it—is a prerequisite to hypnosis success because the subject must take a giant step of faith in surrendering his conscious mind. The reward is the reception of powerful suggestions that may help treatment of physical and mental ailments, suppress pain, fight addictions, encourage resolution of relationship problems, address a variety of other problems and issues, and investigate the paranormal.

4

Hypnosis Techniques

This chapter will explore the techniques of hypnosis. You will learn how hypnotists relax their subjects with soft words of encouragement, relying on personal trust and the power of suggestion to induce them into deep trances.

THREE STAGES OF HYPNOSIS

Remember that hypnosis can help many people. It works well for people who are nervous or slightly neurotic; for people seeking to steady themselves while being considered for an important job or promotion; and for people who are seeing a dentist or for other reasons need a sedative but do not wish to take a chemical agent. The procedure is divided into three stages: light hypnosis, intermediate hypnosis, and deep hypnosis. The stage in which hypnotists have the most success will vary from subject to subject.

Light Hypnosis

In *light hypnosis*, the subject remembers everything that takes place and yet is able to respond to whatever suggestions are made. An alternate is *light suggestion*, in which the subject is talked to in a conversational manner and is generally not asked to lie down. Light suggestion can be valuable if the subject is under stress. It can calm the subject and make her aware of unnecessary anxieties. This

A Note on Self-Hypnosis

Self-hypnosis, also known as *auto-hypnosis,* is similar to that directed by a hypnotist except that this technique cannot include the deep stage. The subject would not be able to come out of deep hypnosis by herself. Self-hypnosis can be dangerous. Only a fully qualified person trained in the technique should attempt it. A verbal command must be established prior to starting the process with firm and specific instructions as to when and how one is to come out of the state of auto-hypnosis.

stage is also useful if the subject is engaged in daily activities that might be interrupted by deeper stages of hypnosis.

Intermediate Hypnosis

In *intermediate hypnosis,* the subject may remember part of what went on, particularly suggestions at the beginning and end of the session, but the recollection will be incomplete. The percentage of what is remembered differs widely from person to person and has a lot to do with the subject's ability to relax.

Deep Hypnosis

Assuming the hypnosis is conducted properly, nothing is remembered from *deep hypnosis,* although there are occasional exceptions. Sometimes, a subject may emerge from deep hypnosis able to recall a few snatches of suggestions, usually from the beginning or end of the session. These memories do not mitigate the effect of the hypnosis.

A QUICK REALITY CHECK

One last word about what hypnosis can and cannot do.

One of the most common reasons given by those unwilling to undergo hypnosis needed for medical or psychological reasons is that they are afraid of surrendering their free will and falling under the "spell" of a hypnotist. This is especially true among women, who often worry that a male hypnotist can make them do whatever he wants. Lurid stories are occasionally told about unethical hypnotists who make unsuspecting ladies undress before them and perform sexual acts. The fact is that a hypnotist cannot make a person behave in a manner contrary to her moral, ethical, and personal beliefs. It is equally true that some people pretend to live by one set of rules while unconsciously harboring a more liberal interpretation of social and moral laws. Among such people there may be some who can be made to undress and perform sexual acts if that is acceptable within their own unconscious minds, and if that unconscious needs to express itself in such a manner. There may be cases where the desire to undress has certain therapeutic values.

Regardless, an ethical hypnotist will always channel her subject's energy and need to express herself in ways that will avoid embarrassment. (See "Hypnotist's Code of Ethics," page 36, for ethical statements that many hypnotists have sworn to follow.)

THE PROCESS OF HYPNOSIS

In all stages, hypnosis is conducted with a series of physical and verbal suggestions. Physical suggestions typically seek to remove or diminish ordinary physical responses to pain or pressure. For instance, a subject may be hypnotized not to feel a pin being inserted into her flesh. Or, she may be made rigid, placed horizontally between two chairs, and made to support the weight of someone sitting on her. These visual tricks are typical of stage hypnosis, although clinical hypnotists occasionally employ them to test the depth of hypnosis in a subject. In the long run, this physical manipulation has little or no therapeutic value.

A state of total rigidity, known as catalepsis, is induced by commands to control certain muscles. The muscles stiffen to the point where the body becomes immovable and capable of resisting great pressure. The danger lies in the possible sudden collapse of the subject if the hypnotic treatment has not been applied properly. It is true that you can be hypnotized to perform physical feats that you cannot normally do, but the hypnotist cannot instill supernatural strength into a subject. She merely awakens what is dormant in the body and mind.

By and large, we are not aware of the potential of our mental

Hypnotist's Code of Ethics

Hypnotists who receive certification from the American Council of Hypnotist Examiners are asked to oblige by the following ethical statements.

- I regard as my primary obligation the welfare of the individual or group served.
- I will not discriminate because of race, color, religion, age, sex, or national ancestry and in my job capacity will work to prevent and eliminate such discrimination in rendering service, in work assignments, and in employment practices.
- I give precedence to my professional responsibility over my personal interests.
- I hold myself responsible for the quality and extent of the service I perform.
- I respect the privacy of the people I serve.
- I respect the rights, desires, and needs of my clients at all times.
- I use in a responsible manner information gained in professional relationships.
- I treat with respect the findings, views, and actions of colleagues and use appropriate channels to express judgment on these matters.
- I practice hypnotherapy within the recognized knowledge and competence of the profession.
- I recognize my professional responsibility to add my ideas and findings to the body of hypnotism knowledge and practice.
- I accept responsibility to help protect the community against unethical practice by any individuals or organizations engaged in hypnotic services.
- I distinguish clearly, in public, between my statements and actions as an individual and as a representative of an organization.
- I support the principle that professional practice requires professional education and continuing education.
- I teach self-hypnosis to my clients/students whenever possible.
- I contribute my knowledge, skills, and support to programs of human welfare.
- I agree that intimate social contact with clients is forbidden for a period of two years from the client's final session.

Visit the American Council of Hypnotist Examiners' website at www.hypnotistexaminers.org for more information.

and physical strength, especially when under stress, and do not realize that sometimes we can perform amazing tasks without the help of hypnosis. A man about to fall from a moving train, for example, may summon abnormal strength in his hands to avoid injury or death. Likely he could not have called on this extra reservoir of strength with conscious deliberation.

Great emotional pressure such as a sudden life-or-death situation stimulates the physical apparatus, drawing from hidden reservoirs of power. The hypnotist can stimulate these power reservoirs artificially. An ethical hypnotist will not do this unless there is good reason for it. For example, a person is about to embark on a strenuous activity, either physical or mental, and is unable to muster the conviction to succeed. A hypnotist may then implant confidence along with a stimulation of the power reservoir through verbal suggestions.

This, however, cannot be done as a matter of routine. A person under the hypnotic suggestion that her ordinary performance will be increased without limit may become ill. However, if her general performance is below par and constitutes a threat to her security, then this kind of treatment can be beneficial. If successful, it will have the same effect as a pep pill, except that it has no side effects and is not habit forming.

Now that you know more about the potential effects of hypnosis, it is time to look at the actual process in detail.

Planting Post-Hypnotic Suggestions

Post-hypnotic suggestions usually relate to vices such as smoking and drinking. For example, a hypnotist may command her subject to feel revulsion whenever she touches a cigarette, or to immediately put down the glass when she takes a drink of liquor. These are reflex suggestions that do not come into play unless the subject picks up a cigarette or takes a drink. Merely suggesting that one no longer wishes to smoke may not stop her from smoking, but this *post-hypnotic aversion therapy* often works.

Hypnosis should be conducted in private. No third person should be present, no matter how close she may be to the subject. The hypnotist obeys the same oath of confidentiality as any med-

ical doctor or other professional dealing in private or personal matters. In most cases, notes are kept of what transpires under hypnosis. When I work with a person, I generally use a tape recorder. I do
not, however, allow the subject to hear a playback of the session
unless and until the treatment or research project is completed.

Creating Ideal Conditions

When creating an environment for hypnosis, the room should be
neither too cold nor too warm. It should not be too brightly lit or
too dark; a dim light is best. The subject should recline on a comfortable couch. Hypnosis can be undertaken with the subject sitting
in a chair, but her neck will invariably become loose and the head
will begin to fall back, causing either an inability to relax or a stiff
neck on wakening. It can encourage relaxation to have the subject
remove her shoes. Clothes should not be tight and confining jewelry should not be worn. If possible, noise should be minimized. This
is not easy in a big city, so I may include a command that the subject not be disturbed by external noises.

Once the subject is comfortable, the hypnotist takes a nearby chair
and begins to relax the subject with a softly spoken introduction:

> *I want you to relax completely now. Empty your mind of all thoughts,
> all problems, and all emotions. You're entitled to a short rest. You are
> here to get that rest and there is nothing that troubles you at the
> moment. Let go more and more. I want you to stretch your body and
> then I want you to close your eyes and listen to my voice. You are to
> listen to my voice only as if it comes to you from a distance. You will
> not be disturbed by external noises. You will only hear my voice
> coming to you from a distance.*

Steadying Nerves

If the subject seems nervous, the hypnotist may suggest breathing
exercises. An example would be simple yoga breathing exercises
consisting of holding the breath and then expelling it three or four
times. After a minute of this, the hypnotist continues:

> *Your arms are getting heavier. Your left arm is getting heavier. Your
> right arm is getting heavier. Your left leg is getting heavier. Your*

right leg is getting heavier. Your entire body feels heavier and heavier and heavier. You are slowly sinking down onto the couch. You are beginning to feel very tired. You are going to take a little nap.

As the hypnotist mentions each part of the body, she may touch it lightly for emphasis. This, however, is the only time the hypnotist should touch the subject. The hypnotist continues:

You will not hear any external noises. If the telephone rings, you will ignore it. You will hear only the sound of my voice coming to you from a distance. You are getting more and more relaxed. You are becoming a little sleepy now. You are very sleepy. You are tired. You want to rest. You want to sleep. All is well. The world is serene, peaceful, and quiet. All is well. You may take a short rest now. No one is going to bother you. You are quite alone, peaceful, quiet, alone.

Feeling Peaceful

The hypnotist should convey serenity, peacefulness, and solitude. A feeling of solitude is important because some subjects cannot relax completely unless they are certain that they are alone.

The first stage, the light stage, will be reached by about fifty percent of those willing to be hypnotized. Subjects afterwards report feeling relaxation, great peace, and a sense of having been asleep for a long time despite being in a hypnotic state for only fifteen minutes. Reaching the first stage usually takes longer than getting to the other two stages, especially when the attempt is made for the first time with a new subject. It is crucial that the hypnotist be patient.

Visualizing Relaxation

Visualizations can be used to get the person to more completely relax, and to take her to where the outer world is dimly recognized but in a way that makes it impossible for the subject to react to it because she is tuning in exclusively to the voice of the hypnotist. I have found that the following visualization works best. In it, the hypnotist suggests that the subject is relaxed, weary, and ready to go to sleep.

You will sleep now for a little while. Nothing will disturb you. You will not be awakened until I awaken you by calling your name. You will close your eyes and keep them closed until you are told to wake up. You will not awaken until your name is called. You are safe, secure, and alone. You have the right to rest now. No one will disturb you. Nothing will interfere with your sleep. As I count to ten you will fall fully asleep. One, two, three, four, five, six, seven, eight, nine, ten.

Trying Again

In many cases, the subject may be too self-conscious or tense to go under immediately. After a few minutes, the subject may sit up and say, "I'm not really hypnotized. I can hear everything you're saying. I just can't go under." This may be perfectly true. In this case, the hypnotist should begin again. The second time, the procedure is familiar and more likely to succeed. Even so, a third attempt may be required. After three unsuccessful attempts, the hypnotist likely will send the subject home and invite her to return another time. Eventually, at least half of all subjects will be hypnotized. Those who simply won't go under may have reasons other than an inability to relax. Often these people do not sincerely believe that they desire hypnosis.

When the subject seems to be asleep following the soothing introduction and the count to ten, the hypnotist may suggest that the subject is now in another place.

The sky overhead is blue and calm. You are in a meadow. The grass is green and fresh. You are sitting down and watching the clouds go by. You are very happy. You are very relaxed. Peace is all around you.

Moving to the Second Stage

Telltale signs of a subject in stage-one hypnosis are regular breathing, a calm countenance, and a relaxed position of the body. The subject's arms and legs should be straight. Under no circumstances should legs be crossed. After a minute or two of this state the hypnotist continues the descent into the second stage:

You will now go down ten more steps toward the water's edge. You're walking through a forest now. The trees are beautiful and tall. It is calm, cool in here. You love the forest. You're walking slowly toward the water's edge. As I count to ten you will be fully relaxed, restfully relaxed, at peace with yourself, all by yourself, all alone in the forest. One, two, three, four, five, six, seven, eight, nine, ten.

At this point, the subject should be even more relaxed and less conscious. Commands are most closely followed in the second stage. Commands given in the first stage are less effective, although it is impossible for the subject to disregard them entirely. With difficult subjects, it is advisable to divide the hypnosis into at least two sessions. On the first visit, the hypnotist should not attempt to go beyond the first stage. The second stage can be entered during the next visit. If the second stage is successful, the third stage can follow immediately. However, a third session may be required to reach the third stage. Any subject who cannot be fully hypnotized in three sessions is not likely to be a good subject.

Waiting in the Forest

Meanwhile, the hypnotist has left her subject in the forest admiring the tall trees and surrounding nature. It is time now for one of two things to happen: Either the subject is taken further, into the third and last stage, or suggestions are implanted while in the second stage. Similar suggestions can be implanted in the second and third stages. For the best results, the hypnotist should try to take the subject further whenever possible. When attempting third-stage hypnosis, the hypnotist guides the subject gently and slowly to the final step.

You will now walk down to the water's edge. You are leaving the forest. You see the water in the distance. You will soon be at the water's edge. The water is warm and pleasant. Overhead the sky is blue. There is a gentle wind caressing you. You feel wonderful. Slowly you walk up to the water's edge. You put your foot into the water to see if it is warm. You like the water. You decide to go swimming. You take your clothes off and you go into the water. You're safe, secure, all by yourself. There's no one here. The only thing you hear is the sound of my voice coming to you from a distance. You will not awaken until I awaken you by calling your name. You will stay asleep restfully, peacefully, quietly. All is well. All is serene. Now you come out of the water. You dry yourself in the sun. As you lie in the sun, the warm light of the sun giving you a feeling of comfort and peace, you begin to relax even more. You will sleep now for a little while. At the count of ten, you will be deeply asleep. One, two, three, four, five, six, seven, eight, nine, ten.

Reaching Deep Hypnosis

Now, the subject has reached the deepest level of hypnosis. At this stage, suggestions can be made to remove undesirable material from the unconscious mind. Let us assume that the purpose of this session is to help the subject stop smoking while instilling a sense of self-confidence that the subject may have been lacking. The hypnotist may proceed by speaking the following:

After you return to consciousness you will no longer like smoking. Whenever you are shown a cigarette you will detest it.

The command is repeated verbatim as the subject is brought back to the second stage and then to the first stage shortly before being awakened. At the same time the hypnotist suggests:

After you return to consciousness you will feel very self-confident. You will feel you can do anything you desire and you will have no anxieties or fears about your accomplishments.

Giving Three Commands

It is standard procedure to implant a command in such a way that the suggestions themselves not be remembered on awakening. Forgetting them, or, rather, being unable to recall them on command, makes them that much stronger while at the same time giving the hypnotist evidence that the session has been productive. Through trial and error, I have found that hypnosis is best suited to giving a subject three definite but short commands, particularly when given at the same time in the same session. The commands can be both positive and negative. This is how the hypnotist may instruct the subject in a three-command session:

You are asleep. You feel fine. You will rest now until I awaken you by calling your name. You will not awaken until your name is called. All is well. You will listen to my words and you will obey all my commands. Even though you are asleep, you will answer if spoken to, and you will answer all my questions truthfully. You will hear nothing but the sound of my voice coming to you from a distance. Now you must rest.

After about thirty seconds of total silence, the hypnotist resumes:

I will give you three commands. You must obey my commands at all times even though you will not remember the exact wording of those commands. My first command is, after you return to consciousness you will stop smoking. My second command is, after you return to consciousness your self-confidence will be increased many times. My third command is, after you return to consciousness you will feel relaxed and happy and rested as if you had slept for many hours. These are my three commands and you must obey them on awakening. Even though you will obey these commands explicitly, you will not remember them. You cannot remember what I have said to you while asleep. You cannot remember my commands, but you must obey them on awakening and for all times. Now you must rest some more.

If there are fewer than three specific requests to be injected into the unconscious mind of the subject, then the third command can be one of general well-being, such as I have just suggested. I should clarify that questioning the subject is not necessary in this kind of therapeutic hypnosis. It may be necessary, however, in the case of regression experiments, especially those dealing with reincarnation. It can also be used in psychic-research hypnosis and forensically to solve crimes. (See "Fighting Crime with Hypnosis," page 44.)

Testing the Depth of Hypnosis

The depth of a hypnosis session directly affects the performance of

Fighting Crime With Hypnosis

The first use of hypnosis to solve a crime was documented in 1845. A clair-voyant was put into a trance to try to identify a thief who had stolen four dol-lars from a store. She described in detail a fourteen-year-old boy and told where he had gone when he left the store. When he was located, he was so startled that he confessed. Other such cases went to court, including one that used "hypnotic influence" as a defense against a murder charge, but by 1897, the Supreme Court of California ruled that evidence discovered through hypnosis was inadmissible.

For decades, hypnosis made little impact on legal proceedings, but that changed in a 1968 case, *Harding v. State.* The victim of a shooting and attempted rape identified her assailant only after she was hypnotized. The Maryland Supreme Court decided that hypnosis was like any other memory aid device, and allowed it without much qualification. That set an important precedent, but things would soon change again.

A more restrictive approach arose from cases in the early eighties, notably *State v. Hurd.* In 1978 in New Jersey, Jane Sell was attacked with a knife while sleeping in her bedroom. She escaped, but afterward, could not recall any details. Put under hypnosis by psychiatrist Herbert Spiegel—who did not interview her prior to the procedure—and with considerable leading, she identified her attacker as her former husband, Paul Hurd, with whom she had two children. It turned out that on the evening before the assault, Jane's cur-rent husband, David Sell, had engaged in a heated phone conversation with Paul Hurd regarding visitation rights. That made Hurd a likely suspect.

In her post-hypnotic state, however, Jane Sell expressed mistrust about her thinking, but Dr. Spiegel and the investigating detective encouraged her to accept her identification to protect her children. She went ahead and iden-tified Hurd as her attacker, and he was indicted and charged with assault with intent to kill, assault with a deadly weapon, possession of a dangerous knife, and breaking and entering with intent to assault.

His defense counsel argued on the basis of *Frye v. US* (1923) that hyp-notically refreshed testimony is inadmissible *per se.* The *Frye* court had decided that anything on which expert testimony is based must be "suffi-ciently established to have gained general acceptance in the particular field in which it belongs." Thus, the lawyer was insisting that hypnosis was not generally accepted as a reliable technique. Furthermore, he argued, Jane

Sell's testimony was tainted by suggestion and coercion. In 1981 the case went to the New Jersey Supreme Court.

Justices Pashman, Clifford, and Sullivan reviewed the issue of whether Sell's testimony was true recall or confabulation. In reaching its decision to bar the testimony, the court came up with the following state guidelines:

1. Witnesses must use a psychiatrist or psychologist trained and experienced in the use of hypnosis.

2. The hypnotist should be independent of, and not regularly employed by, the prosecution, police, or defense.

3. Information given by any party to the action to the hypnotist should be written or recorded and made available to all parties.

4. The hypnosis session(s) should be video- or audio-taped, including pre- and post-interviews.

5. Only the expert and the witness should be present during all phases of the hypnosis.

6. The subject's pre-hypnosis memories for the events in question should be carefully recorded and preserved.

The court determined that Sell's testimony had failed to follow any of the proposed safeguards.

—Excerpt from *Forensic Hypnosis for Memory Enhancement* from the Crime Library® at Court TV®, by Dr. Katherine Ramsland, author, researcher, and assistant professor of forensic psychology at DeSales University.

certain related tasks after the hypnosis has ended. These tasks usually include obeying commands, such as the previous example of getting the subject to quit smoking. Tasks can also be triggered when a certain key phrase or word is heard. The simpler the command, the more likely it will be obeyed. Hypnotists can use this to test the depth of the hypnosis. If the hypnotist wishes to test the depth of her subject's hypnotic state, she may insert the post-hypnotic command to ask for a glass of water as soon as the subject has heard the phrase, "It's rather warm today, isn't it?"

The hypnotist brings the subject out of hypnosis and engages her in ordinary conversation for a few minutes. Casually, she mentions that it is a hot day, and immediately the subject requests a glass of water. When the subject is questioned about her request, she will not know why she asked for water, only that she felt a compulsion to do so.

Post-hypnotic suggestions are natural, unpremeditated expressions. They cannot be suppressed or neglected. If, for some reason, the subject does not wish to say what her unconscious mind urges her to say to satisfy the post-hypnotic command, the urge will become so irresistible that eventually she will blurt out the phrase.

Moving Slowly

It is important that all these words are spoken in a slow, deliberate, soothing tone of voice, neither too fast nor too slow, but always with a feeling of authority as if the hypnotist were a teacher or parent speaking to someone entrusted to her care, which is in fact the truth. Under no circumstances should the hypnotist become impatient, hurry the subject, or raise her tone of voice. The hypnotist must remain calm no matter what, no matter how violent or hostile the reaction of the subject under hypnosis. After about thirty seconds of silence, the journey up the ladder to the first stage begins.

You are very much relaxed now. You are at peace. You will not awaken until your name is called. You will stay asleep until I awaken you. Come forward now and walk through the forest out into the meadow. You will take ten steps forward until you reach the meadow. One, two, three, four, five, six, seven, eight, nine, ten. Now you are in the middle of the meadow. It is green and fresh and you are very happy here. The sun is shining overhead. The air is fresh and there is a gentle wind. You will rest here for a little while.

After a moment, the hypnotist continues:

You will not awaken until your name is called. You will stay asleep until I awaken you. Now you will take ten steps forward toward the surface, but you will not awaken until you are told to do so.

46

Emerging From the Trance

Awakening after hypnotic sleep can be unpleasant or pleasant. Without proper suggestion, the subject may awaken nervously, worrying about what happened during the session. This slightly confused state can be avoided if the hypnotist will add a command that on awakening, the subject will feel relaxed and rested as if she had slept for many hours. After another thirty seconds of silence, the hypnotist slowly takes the subject from the third stage up the ladder to the conscious level. Under no circumstances must this be done quickly or in one steep ascent. This is what the hypnotist may say in leading the subject to wakefulness:

> *You will not awaken until I awaken you by calling your name. You have rested now for a while and you feel wonderful. Now you will take ten steps upward back toward the forest. One, two, three, four, five, six, seven, eight, nine, ten. You are now entering the forest. You admire the tall, cool trees around you. You are very happy. You feel very relaxed. You are now in the forest and you will rest for a little while.*

The three commands are repeated and the order is given that the subject will not be able to remember what was said to her while asleep.

> *At the count of ten you will be fully awake. You will be fully awake at the count of ten. You will feel refreshed and relaxed and very happy as if you had slept for many hours. One, two, three, four, five, six, seven, eight, nine, ten—awaken!*

At this point, I snap my fingers. This is not done for effect. Snapping the fingers creates a sound and a tiny electrical charge that seems to be helpful in releasing the subject from the hypnotic state. After a few minutes of conversation between hypnotist and subject, during which the tone of the hypnotist's voice is altered, shifting to a more conversational level, the hypnotist will probe gently to find out what the subject remembers from the session. The hypnotist will decide at that point whether to recommend another session.

A POSITIVE ATTITUDE CHANGE

At this point, the subject is told to go home and observe any positive changes. Subjects should notice a remarkable change in their attitude. They will find it more difficult to engage in the problem behavior. They will feel improvement in their mental outlook. If self-confidence had been lacking and was instilled during the hypnotic session, the person's relationship with others may change. Friends may wonder what happened to the subject. With the acknowledgment by outsiders that something has changed, the subject herself becomes even more confident that the hypnotic treatment has been successful.

Occasionally, a subject may benefit from additional hypnosis at a later date, especially if great pressures or emotional traumas have occurred. With an occasional session, people can rely on hypnosis to help them over rough spots throughout their lives. Yet it is important to understand that hypnosis is not a crutch on which to lean instead of attempting to live your life yourself. It merely helps bring out your positives and suppress your negatives.

CONCLUSION

Hypnosis has three main levels, each one deeper than the previous one. While in a hypnotic state, the subject's conscious and unconscious are disconnected briefly. This allows the hypnotist to plant verbal and physical suggestions, as well as post-hypnotic suggestions. For the most part, the subject will recall little or nothing of the deeper stages. Typically, hypnosis commands will address the subject's reasons for undertaking the treatment, and immediate results are usually seen.

5

Emotional Hypnosis

Not all hypnosis is induced in a traditional setting in which verbal commands are planted in the unconscious mind of a subject. Sounds, smell, motion, and touch can also create a trance state.

NON-VERBAL COMMANDS

Emotional hypnosis is the term for hypnotic states, or near-hypnotic states, induced by methods other than the verbal commands I have described or the mechanical devices often used by stage hypnotists. The intent is not as clearly defined as it is in ordinary hypnosis, nor is the effect as predictable. In ordinary hypnosis, verbal commands are clear and the channels of communication are sharply defined. In emotional hypnosis, the emphasis is on feelings and emotions. The loosening of the bonds between the conscious and unconscious minds is achieved in other ways.

Rocking to the Music

Sound may cause dissociation. A near-hypnotic state may be created through the effect of certain music; the sound of drums, especially when it is repeated in a monotonous pattern; and songs composed of certain sequences of musical notes.

In Africa, drums have been used to hypnotize people in preparation for initiation ceremonies for the so-called witchcraft fraternities. Candidates are put through a number of ordeals, both physical and mental, and some involve great pain. It is considered desirable for the candidate to be partially numb to what awaits him. Thus, the effect of drum rhythms on his conscious mind produces a state of near-hypnosis, during which he undergoes the required ritual without undue suffering. The emotional impact of Scottish bagpipes may create similar results in some people. Hypnotic effects also are found in some stage effects such as the continual flashing of lights, the movement of lights from one side to the other, and repetitive sounds. (See "The Drums of War," below.)

Creating Trance With Smells

Smell, too, can be used to induce a trance state. Aromatics and incense have long been part of religious ritual in most cultures. A hypnotic effect can be triggered through the inhalation of certain aromatics, many of which are first cousins to the anesthetics used in medicine today. Depending on the specific aromatic, the smell can lull the senses, cause hallucinations, or result in total dissociation of personality.

The famed priestess of the Delphic Oracle in ancient Greece seated herself on a three-legged stool placed over a crack in the earth, from whence sulfur fumes rose. The sulfur fumes caused dissociation in her to the degree that she became entranced and her psychic ability was greatly increased, enabling her to prophesize in a near-hypnotic state.

The Drums of War

"Beware of the leader who bangs the drum of war in order to whip the citizenry into patriotic fervor, for patriotism is indeed a double-edged sword. It both emboldens the blood, just as it narrows the mind. And when the drums of war have reached a fever pitch and the blood boils with hate and the mind has closed, the leader will have no need in seizing the rights of the citizenry, [who] infused with fear and blinded by patriotism, will offer up all of their rights unto the leader and gladly so. How will I know? For this I have done. And I am Julius Caesar."

—Julius Caesar, Roman general, statesman, author, 100–44 BC

Moving Hypnotically

Motion, too, can be used to attain partial or full hypnosis. A short-cut method to full trance among some professional mediums is the rocking motion of head and shoulders, induced generally by a helper rocking the medium in a circular motion. The effect is similar to that of a centrifugal turntable. Standing in a centrifuge results in loss of balance and eventually brings on a hypnotic state.

Dancing as a means of attaining ecstasy was well known to the ancients. Moving around in concentric patterns, changing direction only to avoid vertigo, the dancers would exert themselves until their physical energies were nearly exhausted. At that point, a state of semi-trance was reached in which extrasensory perception might be heightened.

Body exercises are used to reach a state of looseness between conscious and unconscious. An example is runic patterns, in which the person makes certain carefully controlled designs with his body, arms, and legs. Breathing exercises such as those used in yoga can lead to hypnotic states, too, as can holding the breath or prolonged exhaling.

During the Middle Ages, a device known as the *witches' cradle* was used to create a heightened state of awareness. The subject was tied into a kind of straitjacket, which allowed no body movement. The eyes, ears, and nose were covered, with just enough air allowed for breathing. Thus insulated from outside sensations, the cradle was suspended from a ceiling. The subject was completely unaware of his surroundings, incapable of any physical sensations, and thus was forced to rely exclusively on his ESP. Total deprivation of sensory perception leads to a state of dissociation similar to that of the hypnotic state. Whether in a wilderness or a dark room, isolation from other humans will induce a state of dissociation. Hallucinations and visions frequently result.

Feeling the Touch

Touch may induce hypnosis. Dr. Friedrich Anton Mesmer made passes above the bodies of his subjects to bring on a state of hypnosis but did not touch them. (See Chapter 1 for more information on Dr. Mesmer.) When touch is preceded by verbal suggestions,

Teamwork of Mind and Body

Through the deeply meditative practice of Tum-mo yoga, Tibetan monks are able to dry wet sheets placed on their bodies in near-freezing temperatures by raising their skin temperatures seventeen degrees. How the human body can perform this remarkable feat is still unknown, yet it serves as a striking demonstration of the awesome mind-body powers we all possess.

—*Psychology Today,* May-June, 2001

touch can result in total hypnosis. For instance, if the hypnotist conditions his subject by saying, "You'll be fully asleep when I touch you," then on touching the subject, the subject will go to sleep. However, this is not truly the result of the touch but merely the suggested meaning of the touch.

During sexual intercourse, the mingling of two bodies and the natural excitement of touch may lead to a heightened state of awareness of self. In some cases, this can result in a mutual dissociation of personality and the temporary creation of a single personality in the two lovers. A greater possibility of reaching a near-hypnotic state is possible through various stages of mutual discovery, touch, verbalization, vision, and olfactory elements such as lights and aromatics.

Seeing Light and Color

Light and color can contribute to inducing altered states of consciousness. Rapid color changes, for instance, can cause dissociation of personality, while properly cued light effects can cause a person's attention to focus on the light source, resulting in hypnosis. This is how those who employ mechanical tools for hypnosis bring their subjects into trance states.

HYPNOSIS AND DRUGS

The use of drugs in hypnosis is an old and embattled issue. Certain drugs cause the hypnotic state with great ease. Yet, with drug use comes the risk of damage to the subject.

I see no therapeutic value in artificially produced hallucinations. Far from bringing suppressed material to the surface, I believe drug-induced hallucinations introduce foreign elements into both body and emotional personality, which can be confusing rather than clarifying. When drugs are used for medical purposes under professional supervision, there can be no quarrel over their usefulness.

For example, derivatives of LSD (lysergic acid diethylamide) have proven to be valuable aids in treating certain types of mental illness. Yet, the use of hallucinogenic drugs for the sole purpose of escaping reality is not only ill advised. The use of mescaline, peyote, LSD, and the deceptively mild marijuana is also of questionable value when it comes to reaching a desired state of dissociation. The hallucinations resulting from these drugs are artificial and do not bring to the surface any existing symbolic material. They do not lead to psychic awareness, contrary to what some mediums have thought they would do, and they leave a residue of destruction.

Fighting Addiction

Verbal hypnosis can be used as a tool to combat the desire for drugs if the addict truly wishes to be free of his addiction. But hypnosis cannot stand up against the actual chemical push of the drug within the body because the chemical substance reaches the control centers in the brain quicker and with greater impact than the more subtle hypnosis. Remember, no one can be hypnotized against his will, and no one can be helped if they do not want help.

CONCLUSION

Hypnotic or near-hypnotic states can be induced in a variety of non-verbal ways. These ways utilize sound, smells, movement, touch, and sight. Hallucinogenic agents and pharmaceutical drugs can also be used to create a hypnotic state, but are generally not recommended.

6

Beware of Involuntary Hypnosis

We risk losing independence of thought by responding unknowingly to forms of involuntary hypnosis, which seek to plant positive and negative preferences in our unconscious mind.

PUBLIC COMMUNICATION

You won't find the term *involuntary hypnosis* in any book dealing with the subject. Yet, more of us are subjected to this phenomenon than take part in voluntary hypnosis. It is found in various forms of public communication such as advertising, publicity, and propaganda. Its effectiveness depends on its commercial or political messages being received, accepted, and acted on by large numbers of people.

Receiving Negative Messages

In marketing and publicity, products, services, and ideas are described in words and pictures with the goal of having the targeted public favorably inclined toward the message. In some cases, the message is negative—that is, it invites the audience to refrain from certain actions or reject certain thoughts. This is seen, for example, in negative political advertisements. But most advertising invites the audience to respond in a positive way. Outwardly, the message would seem to target the conscious mind. Presumably, we will evaluate the message logically, digest it, dissect it, and either accept or reject it. This all happens on the surface. But let's look a little deeper.

Parallel to this surface reaction, there is a reaction in the unconscious part of the mind. This technique is ancient. The Romans understood the power inherent in certain statements, even ones that were patently false. They believed that no matter how false the message, *semper aliquid hae,* or "something always sticks."

LINGERING MESSAGE

No matter how preposterous the message, and no matter how strongly you may reject that message, some of it will linger in your unconscious mind. In a political context, this will make you doubt the candidate against whom a message is directed. You may believe your conscious thinking is based on purely logical grounds. Yet, the unconscious simply absorbs part of the message whether you like it or not. You have no control over this reaction.

Another example: Consider an advertisement in the newspaper, on television, or on the radio that urges you to buy a product

Much Ado about Nothing

A long-running controversy over involuntary hypnosis began with the 1957 publication of *The Hidden Persuaders* by Vance Packard, a journalist and social critic. He asserted that the media were manipulating the American people with new marketing techniques inspired by *motivational research.* Packard raised public awareness by selling more than one million copies of his book.

That same year, James Vicary, a market researcher from New York, claimed surprising success experimenting with what he termed *subliminal advertising* (from "sub" meaning below and "limen" meaning imperceptible) at a movie theater in Fort Lee, New Jersey. From the projection booth, Vicary flashed onto the screen two messages—"Drink Coca-Cola®" and "Hungry? Eat Popcorn"—every five seconds, using a *tachistoscope,* a device that provides brief visual stimuli.

The message appeared for a few milliseconds, too brief for the theatergoers to consciously register, but apparently long enough to send customers because it will improve your life. The product may be a political candidate, a vacation destination, or anything else that can be verbalized or visually depicted. Logically, you understand this message cannot be trusted. It may even annoy you. Yet, the next time you pass a display of the product, unconsciously you will reach for it ahead of competing products, even as your conscious mind reminds you of having rejected the product's advertising. Your reaction is natural. Something has sunk into your unconscious. (See "Much Ado about Nothing," page 56.)

POWER OF PUBLICITY

Publicity works the same way. By being exposed to the news media, your unconscious receives information bullets that hit their marks regardless of your preference and regardless of your quality evaluation, which might guide your judgment otherwise. Feelings, emotional reactions, religious beliefs, political persuasions, state of health, place of residence—there is nothing that cannot be influenced.

---

to the snack bar. Vicary claimed that the sale of Coca-Cola went up 18 percent and popcorn sales increased 57 percent.

The new marketing technique was controversial and started a national debate that continued off and on for half a century. Despite reports to the contrary, the Federal Communications Commission (FCC) never banned subliminal advertising, but it did issue a statement in 1974 asserting that use of it by the nation's broadcasters was "contrary to the public interest." The FCC has acted on only one complaint. In 1987, it admonished KMEZ-FM, a radio station in Dallas, Texas, for transmitting subliminal "no smoking" messages hidden in songs during the Great American Smoke-Out.

Meanwhile, the validity of Vicary's research was questioned by Dr. Henry Link, president of the Psychological Corporation, according to a report posted on the website www.snopes.com. "Eventually," according to the report, "Vicary confessed that he had falsified the data from his first experiments, and some critics have since expressed doubts that he actually conducted his infamous Fort Lee experiment at all."

Sometimes the message is indirect. When publicity is disguised as a news story, the effect may be even more potent. You may simply hear that people who have bought a certain product have been successful, or happy, or in some way rewarded for their choice. You, or rather your unconscious and uncritical mind, assume that the message lacks an ulterior motive. Typically the unconscious mind accepts information appearing in books, newspapers, and magazines, as well as much of radio and TV programming, as neutral, objective, and factual.

Selling "Hard" and "Soft"

In advertising, there is the hard sell and the soft sell. The *hard sell* is calling the product, service, or idea by name, describing it directly and precisely, and demanding that it be bought, subscribed to, or accepted. Frequently this includes a direct order such as "Buy Now!"

In a *soft sell*, the message focuses on the alleged virtues of the product. These advertisements are less hard-hitting and direct.

"Subliminal advertising does not affect consumer buying behavior, advertising recall, or any other marketplace behavior."

—Jack Haberstroh, author of *Ice Cube Sex: The Truth about Subliminal Advertising*

POLITICAL ACTION

To see what techniques of suggestion can accomplish on a political level, you can look at the hypnotic influence an evil genius, Adolf Hitler, had over the masses in Germany before and during World War II. At the same time, every demagogue and political rabble-rouser is familiar with the potency of the spoken word when it is emotionally tinged and directed toward suggested action on the part of the listener. Another example would be US Senator Joseph McCarthy's aggressive anti-Communist investigations in the early 1950s. He used "guilt by association" as a means to conduct political terrorism. The Wisconsin senator and his allies never directly accused anyone in public life of being Communist. Yet, by suggesting that certain people who were above suspicion had associated with known Communists and had been influenced by them, McCarthy and his allies planted seeds of suspicion in the unconscious minds of the public. Thus, people accused of having associated with a Communist automatically became a suspect, even though in most cases they had done nothing illegal. Nothing lends itself better to political suggestion than guilt by association.

The human mind works best when it is able to associate ideas with objects or objects with people. It works less effectively when dealing with abstraction. Thus, the best teaching methods use visual symbols to convey abstract concepts. In politics, the technique of guilt by association utilizes the inability of the unconscious mind to differentiate between opinion and fact.

Separating Opinion and Fact

Opinions are not the same as facts. Opinions may be based on facts, in which case they are deductions. It is a fact that hundreds of people who had done nothing wrong were thrown out of work during the McCarthy era because of opinions held by their employers about them. These opinions, however, were not necessarily based on facts. Whenever the appeal is made to the unconscious directly, bypassing the conscious mind, there is no need to differentiate between an expressed opinion, no matter how biased, and an established fact.

Most people are not aware of this. They also don't realize that they are being bombarded day in and day out with hypnotic suggestions that may differ in intensity, length, form, and so forth, but are essentially employing identical techniques. These techniques allow the raw, unaltered messages to penetrate our outer defenses—our conscious, logical minds—and reach the unconscious or uncritical portion of our minds.

Invading Our Privacy

Those who shrug off such assaults on our individual independence as mere words having little power are blissfully unaware of the potency of the spoken word. Dr. M. Neumann, the eminent California psychoanalyst, once warned that, "Words are triggers to action." Thoughts are transmitted through words. The power of the news media, advertisers, and others who express opinions in public is far greater than the average person realizes. Our free will and decisions are constantly challenged by suggestions. Not all of them, of course, are evil or even negative, but all do invade our privacy.

YOUR BEST DEFENSE

I do not propose limiting freedom of speech. But I do believe that people should be aware of these pressures, as well as given the tools to defend themselves. How can we safeguard our independent decision-making? How can we insure that our reactions, decisions, opinions, and other expressions are truly representative of our primary desires and not merely echoes of other people's views? There are three ways in which you can deal with the constant bombardment of involuntary hypnosis.

Be More Aware

Critically examine all your decisions and actions while acknowledging these influences. Self-criticism, self-awareness, and a degree of detachment in considering decisions and actions will help you better understand the relationships between your environment and you.

Resist Undue Influences

If you suggest to your unconscious mind that it is being bombarded from the outside, that you don't wish to be unduly influenced, and that your conscious mind is the supreme arbiter of your decisions, then you will find a resistance to outside influences rising within yourself.

Adopt Your Own Philosophy

Develop a philosophy of life that encompasses your fundamental views. This will protect you from undue outside influences. A person without a philosophy of life is an easier target for involuntary hypnosis.

CONCLUSION

Our privacy as well as our intellectual independence is under constant bombardment from involuntary hypnosis in the form of public communication—advertising, publicity, and propaganda. Its effectiveness depends on its commercial, political, or religious message being received, accepted, and acted on by large numbers of people. These messages are both positive and negative. To protect yourself, I suggest that you develop your own philosophy of life that is free of undue outside influences.

7

Love, Sex, and Hypnosis

You may be surprised to learn that hypnosis can help resolve issues of lust, love, and relationships with relative ease. The secret lies in transforming negatives into positives.

MISUNDERSTANDINGS

The difference between happiness and unhappiness in most people is simply a lack of understanding. If that can be overcome, you can transform your relationship from negative to positive, and you'll have an entirely new outlook. It can be that simple. With a positive attitude, you can repair a broken relationship, establish a new one on a strong foundation, or break off an unwanted one. A positive attitude also improves professional output, contributes to better health, and enhances the personality in all aspects.

Love does make the world go round. This is not just a tired catch phrase. The emotional reaching out to another person has a deep psychological significance for the whole person.

> Pains of love be sweeter far
> than all other pleasures are.
>
> —John Dryden, English poet, 1631–1700

I do not suggest that hypnosis be used to tantalize a subject into loving someone whom he does not love consciously. This is not a modern-day replacement for the medieval love potion or a magic trick. But the surface love-hate complex does not always represent the true feelings of the individual. In most cases, unexpressed or unfulfilled love is the result of a lack of communication and/or a lack of being able to express oneself. Conversely, hate is not necessarily the result of a negative attitude of one person toward another. It also can be the result of the same lack of understanding and communication. Here is where hypnosis comes in.

Hypnosis can help a person find a true level of expression by removing layers of false notions that may have accumulated above the true feelings. In reaching down to the unconscious mind and removing the phony attitudes encrusted around the true feelings, these true feelings may turn out to be even more negative than the ones shown to the outside world. In that case, in-depth hypnosis can be extremely helpful in dealing with these inner negative influences. If the feelings uncovered are positive—that is, in the love range of emotions—they will find their own level once they are liberated.

UNEXPRESSED FEELINGS

The more civilized the society we live in, the more complex the values we place on unexpressed feelings. The more distant we are from nature and natural impulses, the more difficult it becomes to allow a continual, uninterrupted flow of emotional stimulation from the mind through the speech mechanism to the outside world.

Restoring Communication

Hypnosis can help. It can do many things for people unable to find expression for their love needs. On the most superficial level, it may be suggested to the subject that he feel free to express himself openly, without shame, inhibitions, or fear. The hypnotist can remove the self-applied shackles of propriety, fear of rejection, and other inhibiting factors that may have stood in the way of the subject's giving free rein to his emotions. In many people, this approach alone will restore the normal flow of communication with others.

Delving Deeper

When the emotional block lies deeper in the unconscious mind, you can consider hypnoanalysis. For this method, the hypnotist first establishes the specific problems. The subject must be willing to discuss his problems freely. The hypnotist then makes a judgment as to whether the issues can be dealt with through hypnosis. This is based on an evaluation of the subject's general characteristics, his relationship to reality, and the level of difficulty he is currently having forming relationships. If the hypnotist believes the subject's own mental block is standing in the way of a successful relationship, he may decide to take the subject down to the third level of hypnosis.

Suggestions planted in the unconscious mind while in this third level should be specific and pointed. The hypnotist will tell the subject that the relationship will improve. The moment the subject awakens from this deep hypnosis, he will feel as though an emotional victory has been won. This will lead to an outer display of new confidence and warmth. Of course, it takes two to tango, and there are no guarantees of lasting success. Therefore, the emphasis is on strengthening the subject's personality. Hopefully, this will result in increased vitality and conviction of emotional success that will be so strong and attractive that the desired partner will be convinced that the relationship is progressing favorably and successfully.

If this sounds complicated and full of hazards, that is because it is. Only a comparatively small number of these cases come to a successful conclusion. But for subjects with severe relationship issues, it may be worthwhile to attempt this form of therapy with a trusted hypnotist. (See "Be Careful Whom You Trust," page 66.)

SEEDS OF LOVE

To instill love in a person through hypnosis is possible only if some seeds of that feeling exist already. To plant alien feelings into one person toward another belongs to the realm of fiction. But there are cases where the seeds of love are so deeply buried in the unconscious mind that a subject is totally unaware. This also holds true

---

Be Careful Whom You Trust

Choosing a hypnotherapist is as important as choosing a primary care physician or any other health care provider. A smart decision is particularly crucial because many hypnotherapists are not licensed by the state in which they practice. Lay hypnotists, for example, are trained in hypnosis but lack any other professional health care training. As a result, these practitioners may have as few as two hundred hours of training, while licensed professionals typically have seen seven to nine years of schooling plus additional internship and residency programs. On its website, the American Society of Clinical Hypnosis offers the following advice for choosing a hypnotherapist.

Gather as much information as you can about your potential hypnotist. Before your first session, find out if he is state *licensed* rather than certified. Keep in mind that certification requires a great deal less education than licensure. Also ask him about his specific degree. If his degree is in hypnosis or hypnotherapy, he is a lay hypnotist. A licensed hypnotist will have a degree

---

with the so-called love-hate syndrome. The emotions of love and hatred are closely related. One can turn into the other under certain emotional conditions, and sometimes the two cannot be clearly separated. Thus, it is possible that a person who hates another might come to love the other person while under hypnotic treatment. The hypnotist has found that the hate in the subject was merely a disguised feeling of admiration and has stimulated the underlying factors rather than the expressed hate. Presto! Hate turns to love.

HATRED AND NEGATIVE FEELINGS

Some people will seek professional help to overcome strong feelings of hatred. Unfortunately, few will seek the help of a hypnotist. Yet, having a logical discussion about the reasons behind the hatred is usually of little help, because while the subject may agree that hatred is undesirable and wish to do something about it, the feeling will most likely persist on an unconscious level.

Hypnosis, on the other hand, can truly absolve these feelings of hatred. For a subject wishing to discard hatred, the hypnotist will probe for underlying causes such as disappointment or hurt in the

in a state-recognized health care profession, such as psychiatry, pediatrics, or dentistry, with hypnosis training in addition to this work.

The only nationally recognized organizations for licensed health care professionals using hypnosis are the American Society of Clinical Hypnosis and the Society for Clinical and Experimental Hypnosis. Membership in one of these groups means that the doctor has already passed certain qualifications. If your potential hypnotist has membership in the American Medical Association (AMA), the American Dental Association (ADA), the American Psychological Association (APA), or the National Association of Social Workers (NASW), he is a licensed doctor and is not a lay hypnotist.

Contact a state or local component section of the American Society of Clinical Hypnosis to determine if someone is a reputable member. If you still have doubts about your hypnotist's qualifications, look for a new one. You can contact either the American Society of Clinical Hypnosis or the Society for Clinical and Experimental Hypnosis for a list of recommended, qualified hypnotists.

past. Once the subject is brought down to the third level of hypnosis, the hypnotist will plant a suggestion that whatever wrong was done to the subject is no longer significant. This is crucial because it gives the unconscious mind a rationale to release its need to express hatred. Then, the hypnotist will fill the void left by the removal of the hatred with a positive suggestion. This suggestion, however, should not be too positive. It may be unwise to suggest that the object of hate become a love object, unless the subject wishes this to happen.

Hatred is so much a part of our ordinary way of life that people often learn to cope with it. At the same time, life is much richer and more fulfilling without the negative influence of hate, and hypnosis can purify the body of these unwanted feelings.

SEXUAL RELATIONS

Hypnosis can play a valuable role in straightening out difficult sexual relations. General hypnosis to relax both partners can be helpful because a relaxed state is conducive to a better sexual relationship. But when the difficulties are of a more specific nature, indepth hypnosis may be needed. If so, one of the following two approaches might help.

Removing the Problem

The first approach should be literal. If a specific sexual hang-up is known, a suggestion can be made at the deepest level of hypnosis that this difficulty no longer exists and that the subject will become capable in the area where he feels failure. Along with the specific, corrective suggestion, the hypnotist may also insert a general suggestion of confidence and wellness.

Long-range, permanent post-hypnotic suggestions can also be made. These suggestions present no danger, provided they are clearly defined. The subject should not be told of them, however, as this may cause him to develop or create new anxieties.

Dramatizing the Situation

The second and somewhat unusual approach to improving sexual relations involves a psycho-dramatic performance on the part of one of the two partners. Under hypnosis, the subject visualizes himself (or herself) as a heroic or symbolic person who brings a satisfying conclusion to the sexual act with his own sexual partner. This visualization is not permanent. Once the subject is convinced that he is capable of satisfactory sexual intercourse with his partner, and has experienced it several times, the hypnotist will dissolve the visualization and return the subject to his true self. At the same time, a suggestion is injected that the success was due to the subject's own sexual powers and expressed feelings, rather than to the imaginary character. In the right situations, this approach is quite successful.

Some relationships may be hypnotic, and they have nothing to do with love and sex. This has to do with the great power of suggestion seen in demagogues, mob leaders, and various other spellbinders. What transpires between these strong-willed people and their audiences is akin to hypnosis even though the audience does not fall under total control. A person subjected to a demagogue's attack may accept suggestions in the areas of politics, religion, and commerce. He may do so quite naturally and unconsciously and even reject any notion that he is under the influence of another mind. He may truly believe the action he takes is of his own accord.

POWER OF DEMAGOGUES

Demagogues do not rely entirely on their magnetic personalities, the power of their speech patterns, or their arguments. They draw on the emotional power of an audience. By shaping pent-up hatreds and wish-fulfillment feelings to their own needs and desires, demagogues are able to gain power from their audiences.

This can work in two directions. You have already read about the potential power of negative orators, such as Senator Joseph McCarthy and Adolf Hitler, on page 58. A great speaker filled with love for his fellow man, on the other hand, can draw on the same powers of a group but project it toward those harboring hostile feelings toward his group. In the 1960s, the so-called "flower children" gave flowers as symbols of love to strangers and passersby. The message said, "Here is a little love from me." If we all did the same, there would be nothing but love in this world. Unfortunately, hippie love actually did very little to diminish hatred in the world.

CONCLUSION

It really is true that love makes the world go round. The emotional and physical bonds we form with others are deeply important, satisfying, and sustaining to us all. The good news is that many love and relationship problems amount to a lack of understanding. It is possible to transform your relationship through hypnosis, by replacing negatives with positives. Of course, there are no guarantees because love is a two-way street. Despite this, hypnotists have achieved much success in this area.

8

Healing Body and Mind

Hypnosis can be an inducing tool for healing, whether to ease the pain of a tooth extraction, encourage the body to repair itself, or untangle more complicated problems of the mind.

PHYSICAL AND MENTAL PAIN

I have discussed the vital aid hypnosis can offer to suppress or alleviate pain during medical and dental procedures. Although hypnosis is an inducing tool rather than a healing agent, it can be a direct agent of healing if properly applied. On the broadest level, hypnosis can work where psychoanalysis fails. It is not a replacement for in-depth psychiatric treatment in psychotic or schizophrenic cases, but it can be useful in the treatment of these conditions if applied by properly trained physicians.

Many people suffer from ailments unique to our modern world, including *psychoneurosis*—mental or personality disorders that are unrelated to known neurological or physical problems and may cause mood swings. Some up-and-down moods are healthy signs that a person is functioning properly on the emotional plane. But when a person thinks she can no longer cope with her day-to-day problems, she may have psychoneurosis and should seek help. She can turn to a psychoanalyst for protracted analysis of dreams and wish-fulfillment images. Or, she may seek hypnosis, which can often cover the same ground in a fraction of the time. When it comes to psychoneurosis, hypnosis can work wonders.

71

Choosing Treatment

The choice as to whether psychoanalysis or hypnosis is the better way to go is a decision the subject must make. There is a pronounced and basic difference in the two approaches. In psychoanalysis, the emotional picture is analyzed in order to see what causes the difficulties. In the end, what emerges may be a totally different personality. With hypnosis, the depth of the unconscious is probed in a similar fashion but without the logical analysis following each session. Instead, negative aspects are removed and replaced with positive suggestions. Hypnosis represents synthesis, rather than analysis; to put it in another way, psychoanalysis takes apart, and hypnosis puts together.

Analyzing the Subject's Issues

Because anxiety states are at the root of all unresolved difficulties—and, thus, psychoneurotic conditions—the hypnotist should deal with these conditions one by one when she has become convinced that they do not have any basis in fact. For instance, it is important to ascertain why a subject is complaining of dizziness while standing on a mountain. Is it because of a particular phobia or fear complex resulting from some unresolved difficulty, or is it the result of purely physical conditions such as poor circulation or Ménière's syndrome—a loss of balance caused by a disorder of the inner ear? If it is not a result of physical conditions, the hypnotist should address the phobia or fear complex that is causing the problem. In this case, the hypnotist may suggest, in so many words, "You have been feeling dizziness because you doubt your own success in the future. You will no longer feel dizzy no matter how high you stand. You will feel relaxed and well. There is nothing to worry about. You are well."

TREATMENT PATHS

Hypnotic treatment can reach the subject on two levels.

Dealing with Anxiety

In dealing with symptoms of anxiety, the hypnotist can counteract

Hypnotism in Dentistry

According to the American Society of Clinical Hypnosis, the following are ten ways that hypnotism can potentially help a patient with dental problems.

1. Modifies patient's behavior.
2. Relaxes the patient and controls her anxiety.
3. Rids the patient of unnecessary fear.
4. Helps patient overcome undesirable habits related to dental problems.
5. Causes effects of analgesia and pain control; works as an anesthesia.
6. Prevents gagging and nausea.
7. Controls saliva and bleeding.
8. Creatives visualization for healing.
9. Desensitizes before treatment.
10. Assists with self-image, self-esteem, and confidence.

the negative feelings by suggesting they do not affect the subject and by injecting calming suggestions. This will take care of the symptoms but not the underlying causes. To find the causes, the third stage of hypnosis is necessary. At that point, it is advisable for the hypnotist to open up the subject, so to speak, and command her to speak freely of her anxieties and problems. During this process, the patient should not be woken and her eyes should remain closed.

This is similar to the method used in regression experiments done in reincarnation research. If the subject is hypnotized properly and brought down to the third level of hypnosis, she will not wake up even though she will be speaking freely and at great length about her emotional problems. Then, the hypnotist will remove negative factors, give positive commands, and see to it that the confession made under hypnosis is not remembered later. In rare cases, remembering is desirable for therapeutic reasons. The hypnotist must decide what is best for each individual.

Dealing with Physical Disorders

In addition to dealing with anxiety states and other emotional factors, hypnosis can be useful in the treatment of physical disorders. Suggestion can stimulate glandular action and the healing processes within the body when an injury has been suffered. By implanting belief in rapid recovery, hypnosis can actually cause a chain reaction of self-stimulation in the patient. (See "Study Supports Medical Hypnosis" below and "Hypnotism in Dentistry" on page 73.)

UNREASONABLE INSANITY

The problem with treating any form of insanity relates to the inability of the hypnotist to reach the subject. A truly insane person knows no reason. Yet hypnosis is dependent on cooperation between hypnotist and subject, and logical thinking is required in the early stages. No hypnotist, therefore, can get through to a truly

Study Supports Medical Hypnosis

James H. Stewart, MD, of Jacksonville, Florida conducted a study of hypnosis's role in medicine. He studied clinical trials in which hypnosis was used to aid in the treatment of various medical conditions.

Dr. Stewart discovered that hypnosis appeared to have positive effects in the treatment of allergies, eczema, irritable bowel syndrome, peptic ulcers, high blood pressure, obesity, chronic ringing of the ears, chronic fatigue syndrome, and impotence, among other conditions.

A database of medical knowledge for consumers, www.medicinenet.com, reported Dr. Stewart's study. It noted, "Many of the diseases and conditions for which hypnosis has been reported to be beneficial can only be partially treated by the therapies and medicines we currently have available. It therefore seems that since hypnosis affords a relative harmless treatment option, its use as a complementary treatment should be further explored by doctors and other health-care providers."

While Dr. Stewart's report described hypnosis as "a relative harmless procedure," it did warn that possible side effects include "headaches, dizziness, nausea, anxiety, and even panic."

schizophrenic person. But there are borderline cases of partial schizophrenia as well as cases of a person being only temporarily insane and going back and forth between rationality and irrationality. During remissive periods, a hypnotist may reach the unconscious of the patient. In this case, the subject should be asked to speak freely by what is known in psychology as *free association* and thus empty her unconscious of all accumulated pressures. Follow-up treatment will most likely be necessary.

"Worry is a thin stream of fear trickling through the mind. If encouraged, it cuts a channel into which all other thoughts are drained."

—Arthur Somers Roche, author, screenwriter, 1883–1935

Seeking Outside Help

Not all physicians working in this field are good hypnotists, and it is therefore desirable that they draw on hypnotists outside medicine to assist them. Some forms of mental illness, if not the majority, are due to biochemical imbalances in the system. In some cases hypnosis may start a reaction to correct that imbalance, while in other people the hypnotic suggestion implanted in the unconscious mind of the schizophrenic can yield inhibiting factors, improvements as to the reality gap during attacks, or renewed interests in outside activities. This can be a major breakthrough when dealing with patients suffering from total-withdrawal symptoms.

Hypnosis cannot cause deterioration of the schizophrenic condition. If it works, it is beneficial. If it does not work, nothing is lost.

Timing the Treatment

Deep depressions and exaggerated elation-depression curves, a condition called *bipolar disorder,* lie within the spectrum of psychoneuroses. During the depressed state, hypnosis is neither advisable nor possible. At the height of the elated condition, most subjects feel they do not need it. For this reason, it is advisable to

attempt hypnosis for those suffering from bipolar disorder somewhere during the climb up toward the elated position but before the
peak is reached. During these times, the subject seems natural and
outwardly adjusted to reality. The patient should present no special
difficulties going under hypnosis.

Once the third stage of hypnosis is reached, the hypnotist must
allow the subject free-association confessions without permitting
her to awaken.

Hypnotic treatment for bipolar disorder is somewhat complicated. After all, the hypnotist has to suggest that things are neither
as black nor as white as the subject may take them to be at various
times during the bipolar curve. It is best for the hypnotist to suggest the subject perform some practical, useful activity in which the
elated state may provide enthusiasm while the depressed state is
not too damaging so long as the subject sees progress in her activity. The hypnotist can suggest, therefore, that the therapeutic activity chosen will lead to a successful conclusion.

Frequently, subjects with bipolar disorder develop intense hostility feelings toward people they believe are responsible for the
negative phase of manic depression. To forestall this, under the
right circumstances, the hypnotist may be able to single out these
people and instill a feeling of love or respect for them. When the
moment of descent arrives again, the hypnotic suggestion or post-
hypnotic suggestion, if that is preferred, will start to work. The suggestion will greatly alleviate the feelings of hostility if not entirely
removing them.

The Advantage of Hypnosis Over Drugs

In hypnosis, we are dealing with mind-to-mind communication.
Thoughts formulated in the mind of the hypnotist and expressed
through her verbal commands infiltrate the mind of the subject. If
these suggestions remain there, nothing will be accomplished. For-
tunately, however, humans are so complicated that something
entering the mind must filter on into the nerve centers and through
them into the body. At the same time, all thoughts received by the
mind stimulate the emotions and cause what we have come to call
feelings.

Thus, the hypnotist operates on two levels simultaneously. Her suggestions cause actions through mind and body, and feelings through the emotions. Healing only occurs if both the mind-body system and the emotional personality are affected simultaneously and from the same source. To deal with one without touching the other will not yield positive results. Hypnosis is therefore a prime instrument of healing and quite superior to conventional chemical agents because it leaves no residue, has no side effects, and reaches the very center, where all activities originate. On the other hand, hypnosis requires cooperation of the subject, while chemical agents do not.

CONCLUSION

Hypnosis can be helpful in helping repair malfunctions of the body and mind. Through the power of suggestion, a subject's self-healing powers can be stimulated, and issues that inhibit healing can be resolved. This requires skill and patience on the part of the hypnotist and cooperation on the part of the subject.

9

Mysteries of Silent Hypnosis

ilent hypnosis utilizes the extraordinary powers of mere eye contact, telepathy, and emotion-laden symbolic objects or religious relics to create frenzy or mob action.

THE EVIL EYE

I wrote earlier that the superstitious belief in the evil eye, as still exists in parts of southern Europe and Latin America, is not based on fact. The evil eye cannot hex people. But there is more to the evil eye than mere superstition. Belief in this power goes back to antiquity and is based on the extraordinary power inherent in the human eye. The ancients referred to the eyes as mirrors to the soul because through them one connects with another world and through them stimuli from the outside world enters the unconscious.

Channeling Emotion Through Eyes

Physically speaking, the eyes are channels through which light rays reach the brain in order to convey the scenes from the outside. Because the pupil creates a narrow channel, light enters the eye as a beam. But the traffic goes both ways. The eyes also cast a beam from one person to another. This beam, however, is invisible and consists of emotionally tinged, tiny particles of energy derived from the mind.

This is not a figment of the imagination. Almost everyone has experienced the odd sensation of being stared at and has turned around to find someone staring. Intense glare causes uneasiness. The expression "something about his eyes" is a common way of describing a person's superior influence due to unusual eyes.

During the Renaissance, a method of painting eyes was developed by which the eyes of a portrait would appear to follow the viewer as he walked past them. Large posters showing Uncle Sam were responsible for much success in the recruiting campaigns of World War I. The cosmetics industry puts great emphasis on the eyes, enlarging them, framing them, and otherwise drawing attention to them.

Warding off Evil

Jewelry representing the human eye has become popular among those interested in the occult. Ancient Egypt recognized the significance of the eye in fashioning the popular *Eye of Osiris*, which supposedly warded off the evil eye if worn around the neck.

The third eye is sometimes referred to in esoteric studies as the seat of higher wisdom. There is a highly improbable account of how a Tibetan lama had a hole drilled into his forehead so as to permit the third eye to open.

Making Eye Contact

It appears that emotional beams can be sent forth between the eyes of human beings or even between humans and animals.

Everyone has been in a situation where he has seen someone across a crowded room at a gathering of strangers and wanted to make the acquaintance of that person. By nature and because of our social upbringing, we are not likely to go over and introduce ourselves. Women in particular will not do this. Yet, one person may look at the desired person, and perhaps their eyes meet. Something happens. If they are both in tune—that is, if they both wish to meet each other across the social barriers—the very fact of their meeting "eyeball to eyeball," so to speak, will establish a bridge between them. Literally, something has passed from eye to eye. This something is not merely imagination or wishful thinking. It represents a tangible exchange of energy.

An animal's eyes have the power to speak a great language.

—Martin Buber, Jewish philosopher, 1878–1965

Tiny particles have traveled from one pair of eyes to the other, and back. In this exchange of energy, the emotionally tinged energy particles of the first person become intermingled with those of the receiver. On the return trip, the sender receives part of the emotionally tinged particles of the receiver. A silent bond has been established. Inevitably, within minutes, they will smile at each other and one or the other will approach to start a conversation. But the initial contact has been a silent one.

By the same token, a particularly strong-willed and gifted person with unusual eyes may reach out to another person or even large groups of people. Without saying a single word, he may be able to bring them all under his influence. This influence, to be sure, will not go all the way to total hypnotic immersion, but the first or suggestive state of hypnosis can be reached merely by the exchange of glances between the gifted individual and another person.

A popular game among children is staring each other down. Some can withstand being stared at for great lengths of time, but most cannot. This phenomenon takes place in the animal world, too. Try staring a cat in the eyes. Inevitably he will run away. These are all results of the power that can be found in eye contact.

MOB ACTION

Silent hypnosis may go beyond holding another person or group of people under a spell. Commands can be issued. These are not spoken commands but rather thought commands, and are always simple and direct. This is telepathy, of course, but a form of telepathy made possible through establishment of a hypnotic bond between sender and receiver. When it is beneficial, there need be no reason to shun it. But it can be used for negative purposes. During political rallies or exhortations of fanatical religious prophets, influencing a crowd by this method can lead to mob action.

A hypnotist employing silent hypnosis should have positive purposes, however. The method is applied in the following examples.

Removing Distractions

It is important to make certain that there are no diversions in the room in which the experiment is to take place. Attention must focus solely on the hypnotist. Whether an individual or a group, the audience should be comfortable and relaxed, both mentally and physically. Then, the light should be lowered, placing the audience in a condition of semidarkness but leaving the hypnotist's face clearly visible.

After one or two minutes of eye contact, maintaining a steady gaze, the hypnotist should blink and immediately send forth his first command—silently, of course. This must be specific and brief, such as, "Let us stretch." The hypnotist awaits reaction to the suggestion. He can repeat it several times telepathically. He then empties his mind as much as he can.

Within minutes he should see his audience beginning to stretch. If it is one person, the transmission is even easier. If a group is involved, the response rate may not be a hundred percent but it should include a large portion of the audience.

As soon as the hypnotist is aware of his initial transmission's success, he will continue by staring at his audience again for a moment and then transmitting a second message. This may be somewhat more complicated, such as, "Let us sing." Prior to starting the experiment, the hypnotist explains that the audience should feel free to do whatever it feels compelled to do, no matter how unusual or unorthodox the behavior. This instruction is crucial because otherwise the audience may receive the telepathic message and suppress it because it seems out of place.

Training Animals

Silent hypnosis can be applied to animals, especially in training. Although much more primitive in their mind-body makeup than humans, animals are conscious of feelings to the degree that they can understand their masters' desires, provided these desires are expressed in simple and direct ways appropriate to the animal world.

You cannot teach an animal something it is not ready to learn. You also cannot teach human tricks to an animal. You can, however, use silent hypnosis to teach an animal to lie down, come to you, be quiet, and respond to other commands. To reinforce the eye-to-eye contact between trainer and animal, gently stroke the animal's head just above his nose. This creates a state of relaxation that sometimes leads to partial hypnosis merely by the rhythmical pattern of strokes.

Silent hypnosis does not require the release used with verbal hypnosis. When it wears off, the subject enters the normal, non-hypnotized state gradually and without any residue.

RELIGIOUS CEREMONIES

Silent hypnosis is also used during certain emotionally tinged religious ceremonies. In addition to the verbal hypnosis in some sermons or religious rituals, the fixed presence of ritual objects and even the construction of the temple or church may have hypnotic effects on the worshiper. The power of suggestion rests not only in people but also in objects created by people.

Religious symbols and symbols can be focal points and concentration devices carefully designed to catch the attention of a potential subject so that the subject will fall under the influence of the ideas represented by the symbols. In rare cases, fixing one's eyes on a holy relic, as some worshipers are taught to do, can create a partial dissociation of personality that can lead to religious frenzy. This is as old as man's desire to express himself emotionally.

The earliest cave dweller knew how to distill emotional connotations of the deity into simple, powerful designs. The Egyptians brought this to the height of sophistication, when countless symbols represented different aspects of the deities. To dismiss such symbolic designs merely as fanciful and lacking any power is disregarding the known results.

People are influenced by symbols of this kind when they are prone to seek emotional guidance from outside stimuli rather than from within. The majority of people need this outside stimulation to bring order into what otherwise might become emotional chaos. As long as people need the stimulation of others to guide them, teach them, or point them in a desired direction, there will be interplay between leaders and followers.

POWER OF SUGGESTION

Whether openly or secretly, suggestion plays a vital role in the development of personal relationships. It is my belief that only a small number of people are capable of generating original thoughts. Most humans follow or interpret the thoughts of others. If this was otherwise, and every one of us was in charge of our own creative processes and independent of all others, life would be quite different. Total slavery and total freedom are equally unnatural. Everything in nature is interdependent rather than independent.

Hypnosis shares with magic the distinction of having two faces. There is no such thing as black magic or white magic. There is only magic, performed by people with dark purposes and performed by those with constructive aims. Thus it is with hypnosis. If the results of hypnotic suggestion are undesirable, the fault lies not with the method but with those applying it. Hypnosis is not a parlor game, a power tool, or a panacea. It is one of the most natural and valuable aids by which humans can understand themselves better, as well as correct the evils of civilization and estrangement from that same nature that has given us the power of hypnosis since the dawn of time.

CONCLUSION

Bridging the gap between ancient practices and modern experiences, silent hypnosis can include powerful symbolic objects, emotional eye contact, induced mob action, and religious frenzy.

10

Hypnosis and the Sixth Sense

Our unconscious mind is where we receive our psychic input. Hypnosis opens a direct channel to our unconscious mind, and is therefore important in the investigation of the phenomena of extrasensory perception (ESP).

OPEN DOOR TO MIND

Hypnosis is essentially a wedge that opens the door to the unconscious mind by removing the outer layers of the conscious. This permits faster and deeper exploration of subconscious levels where ESP phenomena function. Hypnosis is an instrument that is applied equally but with mixed results to good and bad subjects, to psychic persons, and to those who have little ESP. The results of hypnosis in psychic-research cases vary greatly with the psychic ability of the subject.

Most professional mediums do not need hypnosis or even light suggestion to "go under"—that is, enter a trance. They are able to put themselves into the required state. A few may require hypnosis to get started, especially if they're performing before a large audience or under unusual circumstances.

While a professional medium may be hypnotized at the outset of an investigation, it does not follow that she is therefore under the influence of the hypnotist for the entire session. To the contrary, the hypnotic control ceases as soon as she has reached the psychic level.

At this point, external material is permitted to enter her unconscious and be brought to the surface through her vocal chords. At the end of the session, the medium will emerge from the trance state without help. Occasionally the hypnotist may relax her afterwards if remnants of the trance material linger in the medium's personality. But this is usually a cleansing process and has no relationship to the material itself or its validity.

PSYCHIC POWERS

Hypnosis is invaluable in increasing the power of a psychic person. By removing doubts about her ability through suggestion, the hypnotist is able to create a greater sense of self-confidence and make the medium a better receiver. But there is more to hypnotic treatment than the actual suggestions. Implanting these commands expands the subject's psychic consciousness, and something within the person's emotional self becomes stirred up. To increase a subject's psychic powers, the hypnotist has two options. She can either plant hypnotic suggestions to increase psychic abilities, or she can concentrate on removing doubts to create a vacuum into which comes additional psychic capacity.

Treating Mediums

I have treated several professional mediums in this manner. These people came to me after they had started on careers. They were not beginners, but felt that their sixth sense could be improved. I gave simple commands in two or three initial sessions. Afterward, these subjects moved to a higher level in their professional careers. Immediately, more of their clients were satisfied and remarked on the accuracy of their psychic readings. This could not be merely attributed to increased self-confidence. They could not understand why they were doing so much better after the treatments but accepted the fact they were, and came back from time to time for a "booster shot."

These follow-up sessions were helpful, too, whenever these professional psychics experienced personal depression, became ill, or had been upset by an emotional event. Afterwards, their powers were once again restored, and they would go for months without the need for any additional treatments.

TELEPATHIC COMMUNICATION

Telepathy, a state similar to hypnosis, is a channel of communication between two minds. An individual can enter into this state without outside help as it occurs naturally under certain psychic conditions. It does not matter whether the people are close together or far apart. Telepathy seems to occur when there is some emotional need for it. It can be induced under certain test conditions, but spontaneous telepathy is more powerful. This is not surprising. True emotional emergencies cannot be reproduced in a laboratory.

Sensing Urgency

In telepathy, thoughts, words, images, and anything else that exists conceptually in a mind can be transmitted to another person's mind. Whether the recipient is open to the message depends on a number of circumstances, both mental and physical. The element of urgency is almost always necessary, according to data from respectable psychic researchers worldwide. Frequently, this urgency is coupled with the inability for one person to communicate with another through ordinary channels. Sometimes telephones don't work or the exact whereabouts of a person are unknown. When ordinary means have failed, the telepathic message may succeed.

A classic case is the communication of images of danger between two loved ones separated by distance. Another is a person sensing strongly that a family member is in mortal danger. In other cases, it may be merely a hunch or a less specific awareness of the danger. Generally, telepathic transmissions occur instantaneously, or nearly so. Follow-up research in many cases has verified that the danger sensed by the telepathic people did, in fact, exist.

Losing the Way

In some cases, recipients find themselves in a state of temporary dissociation when they receive a telepathic message. For instance, a daughter may be walking down a street or sitting in her kitchen. Suddenly, she feels as if she is someplace else and she senses that her father is nearby and in danger. This impression may be felt for as briefly as two or three seconds. During this time, she is dimly aware of her ordinary surroundings, which seem flat and unreal, as if she were looking at them through a thick glass. Her own sensations are temporarily muted while her feelings for her father are strong and immediate. This state of partial dissociation of personality occurs often, but not always, when telepathic communication of an emergency nature takes place. Because it is of short duration, there is no time to react to it or do anything about it.

CONCLUSION

Extrasensory perception (ESP) takes place within the unconscious mind. Its ability to temporarily detach the unconscious mind from the more practical, logical conscious mind lends itself as a vital tool in the investigation of a variety of little understood psychic phenomena, and may be the key to opening doors to unknown worlds.

11

Reincarnation and *Déjà vu*

Hypnosis is used to facilitate *regression*, in which a hypnotized subject is gradually led back in time beyond the threshold of his birth to investigate the possible existence of a former life.

NEW LIFE AFTER DEATH

When I was on a publicity tour for *Born Again: The Truth about Reincarnation*, interviewers who had not bothered to read the book kept introducing me as "the man who hypnotized people to find out who they had been before." Nothing could be further from the truth. I have never administered hypnosis for the sole purpose of searching out a possible previous life.

Requiring Careful Research

Reincarnation, the return after death to a new human life, is a subject requiring high standards for scientific research. In many areas of the so-called occult, the line between the scientifically respectable and the colorfully occult becomes slightly indistinct. This is regrettable because, as a result, it tends to blur the difference between respectable research and gypsy fortune-telling.

The oldest of all Western religions, the so-called "old religion" of the Stone Age, held reincarnation as a basic tenet of the faith. To be born again with and near a loved one after one's lifetime was the greatest reward possible. In Eastern civilizations, reincarnation is an accepted tenet as well. In India, belief in *transmigration*—a return to another life in animal form—as well as in reincarnation exists in large segments of the population. (I have personally investigated many cases suggesting that reincarnation takes place but none to prove the existence of transmigration.)

Connecting With Religion

All religions contain elements of reincarnation belief. In Judaism, there is reference to the prophet Elias and the need for him to "come again" before the Messiah arrives. In early Christianity, there are references to being "born again," meaning reincarnated.

It appears the church later found it necessary to deny the concept of reincarnation in order to make the idea of a universal resurrection based on guilt and reward more logical and acceptable, and "born again" was altered to mean the acceptance of Jesus Christ into one's life.

Belief in reincarnation was all but eliminated by the state-church alliance in the Middle Ages but it reemerged in Europe during the sixteenth century, when religious sects such as the Anabaptists hinted at belief in rebirth.

Studying Reincarnation

During the scientific awakening of the nineteenth and the early twentieth centuries, reincarnation was dismissed or relegated to Eastern philosophy. Only in the past fifty or so years has serious scientific research into reincarnation been undertaken.

The pioneer in this field is Dr. Ian Stevenson, a psychiatrist at the University of Virginia medical school in Charlottesville, Virginia. Dr. Stevenson has written a number of articles and a book, *Twenty Cases Suggestive of Reincarnation*. In *Born Again*, I list another twenty or so cases I investigated. Dr. Stevenson and I arrived at parallel conclusions: Reincarnation does occur. I believe we all are reincarnated at various times and under differing circumstances, but without being aware of it. Memories of prior lives exist only in exceptional cases.

Triggering Past-Life Memory

In examining the exceptional cases in which memories of past lives were retained, I found that every one contained the common element of a life cut short by accident, illness, or misfortune. These individuals were prevented from fulfilling their destinies in their previous lives. For whatever reason, these people retained memories of their reincarnation as they entered new lives. These memories are fragmentary. They seem to be in the nature of a partially erased tape-recording in which snatches of previous conversations can still be heard.

Hypnosis should be undertaken for research only if there are conscious memories hinting at possible reincarnation in a subject who wishes to delve into the question of his previous lives. In my experience, conducting research coldly merely as a matter of curiosity, no matter how well intentioned or how serious, is neither good science nor likely to yield results. Although thousands of people have requested regression, such requests should not be granted unless there is already some conscious indication of reincarnation material. (See "Remaining Impartial," page 92.)

REINCARNATION CLUES

There are several characteristics that are common in what some researchers believe to be reincarnation memories. Let's look at these factors.

Sensing Something Strange

At any time in a person's life, he may develop a strange feeling of being or having been someone else. This feeling may come on suddenly or gradually. In part, the feeling is that of being out of step with his family and surroundings. It must be pronounced and specific, but not simply a result of dissatisfaction with his life. He may be unable to live according to his own background and upbringing or, conversely, he may discover skills, habits, desires, and tendencies that are totally alien to his current status, background, and surroundings.

For example, a person of Anglo-Saxon background brought up

Remaining Impartial

It is important that a hypnotist be objective during a session or investigation. To do this properly, he should enter with no expectations, assumptions, or prior knowledge about this particular situation. Any professional worth his salt will not have acquainted himself with the details of a case until after he has completed his investigation.

One time, for example, my subject was a medium. Together we went to a so-called haunted house. I hoped to pick up something from the past or to allow the "resident entity" to speak through his vocal chords. Of course I did have a general idea about what was going on but my knowledge was fragmentary, barely enough to decide whether the case was worth investigating. I made certain the medium had no information about the case or the location of the house, and that neither him nor myself discussed the case with anyone. This made it impossible for the medium to fabricate a story. Whether or not the material obtained through the medium was detailed enough that it could be verified was a decision that I or an independent researcher—and certainly not the medium—had to make.

in rural America without ever having traveled abroad may suddenly discover he has an intense interest in Turkish culture. It may become so pronounced that, on hearing a Turkish song, he will break into a dance, performing steps that he could not possibly know. Or, with no logical explanation, the person may know the words of a song in the Turkish language. This may be followed by an intense desire to go to Turkey and relive certain dimly felt past events. If such a person has the opportunity to follow his inner urgings, he might find himself in new surroundings that seem completely familiar, recognizing unknown places, and saying or doing things completely alien to his personality and character.

Having Recurring Dreams

Dreams that occur repeatedly in much the same manner, different only in small details, may suggest reincarnation. Occasionally, a recurrent dream may warn of impending disaster, but most of them—especially those set in the past—suggest past lives and are most valuable in reincarnation research. With such dreams, it is important to determine if the subject sees himself in the dream. If he does, he must then determine if he looks like his current physical self or appears to be in another body. In particularly significant cases that suggest a connection to reincarnation, the person sees himself but in a different physical form.

Unlike ordinary dream material, psychic dream material is not quickly forgotten on awakening. Occasionally the recurrent dreams have *continuity,* which means that subsequent dreams extend and advance the story as if it were a film being run inside the subject's mind.

Sensing the Familiar

The third indication of reincarnation is called *déjà vu.* This is a French psychological term meaning "already seen." An example is a person who walks into a house for the first time, but immediately recognizes his surroundings, knowing what is upstairs and what can be found in the rooms. Another example is a soldier who arrives in a foreign city yet tells his buddies what lies around a certain corner and leads them as if he has been there before, although he has not. Or, someone might have a sudden feeling of saying or hearing something that he has said or heard before—somewhere, someplace—but is unable to recall the exact circumstances. This feeling of "it has happened before" can be terrifying at times and may create brief dissociation, which passes quickly and without aftereffects. *Déjà vu* is among the most common of all ESP phenomena. Almost everyone has had an incident of this kind at one time or another.

However, most *déjà vu* incidents are not connected with reincarnation. To the orthodox psychiatrist a *déjà vu* experience is simply a case of "opening a false memory door"—that is, somehow crossing wires in the brain and causing an erroneous impression. This explains nothing. It merely labels an unusual phenomenon without seeking a deeper explanation. I believe the explanation of parapsychologists is more plausible: Most *déjà vu* phenomena are brief precognitive flashes that are ignored when they occur. Later, when the foreseen event becomes a real one, we remember that we have seen or heard it before. This comes as a shock to us, although it is a perfectly natural phenomenon.

The Time Slip

Another phenomenon associated with reincarnation memories is the *time slip*. This involves a person's sudden dissociation in terms of time and/or space. A person might drive down a street and suddenly find himself in a different town at a different time. His own reactions are completely normal. He realizes that he is out of step with his surroundings and becomes curious about it. He makes inquiries as he goes along, speaks to what appear to be ordinary, three-dimensional people, and receives answers. But there is a strange atmosphere surrounding the scene, as if he and the other people are frozen in time.

Just as suddenly he returns to the present. Afterwards, he remembers details. The individual believes that the people he talked to were real people and that his experience occurred on a three-dimensional, physical level.

Study of the time-slip phenomena is relatively new. Much more research will have to be done before it is understood. Time-slip experiences seem to hint at the ability of some people to travel through time. It is not clear whether this occurs on a familiar, physical level or in another dimension.

The time-slip experience may be explained in two ways, depending on the nature of the phenomenon.

Recalling Previous Life

The time slip episode may have been the recollection of a previous life, brought on by being in the location where that life was lived. One woman went to Florence, Italy and had a similar experience. She recognized a certain street she never had seen. As she walked down that street, her surroundings suddenly changed, and she found herself back in the Renaissance period. Briefly, she relived a scene from the earlier time. Then, just as suddenly, she returned to the present where her husband was startled to see her appear stunned as if having received a physical blow. The entire incident had taken only a few seconds. (For another example, see "Married to a Civil War Correspondent," page 95.)

94

Reading the Past

Other episodes can revolve around the person's psychic ability to read past events where they occurred. This is called *psychometry*. Over a period of time, I investigated certain historical spots with competent trance-mediums. Together, we would reconstruct past events where they had originally occurred. Where reincarnation memory of the person begins and psychic ability ends can be difficult to determine. If the person does not see himself in the scene he relives, he may be having a psychic experience—that is, reading an imprint from the past that does not apply to him personally. But when the person clearly recognizes himself in the scene, even in another body, reincarnation is a more likely explanation.

Married to a Civil War Correspondent

All my life I've been interested in the Civil War and writing. I've also always had dreams of people I don't know and houses I've never seen. I visited a hypnotherapist last year who through regression took me back into a past life.

It was the year 1863. My name was Marian. I was a forty-year-old wife and mother of three children—Eloise, nineteen, Robert Jr., seventeen, and Beth Ann, twelve. My husband, Robert, was a Pennsylvania newspaper writer who was currently serving as a correspondent in the Civil War.

I was very upset because our son had signed up for duty without permission. I remember wishing that my husband was there to straighten things out. It was a hot day. I kept telling Eloise to loosen the baby's clothing. Eloise was already married and had a baby. During the regression, I began to cry. I kept saying that my nephew had been killed early on in Virginia, and I was scared for Robby. Finally, right before she brought me back, the hypnotist found out that I had lived three times before the present.

The first time, I was an African man who died after being bitten by a poisonous snake. My second life was also as Marian, in Pennsylvania. As Marian, I eventually died a natural death. My third life was as a nine-year-old child, Sara. I had tuberculosis and was living near Boston in the early 1920s. My mother and stepfather, a kosher butcher, sold everything, and the entire family moved to Arizona for my health. I died at fourteen.

—"Maria," posted on www.healing.about.com, a health and fitness website, August 2003

How do I know all this? Frequently critics ask me how I can be sure that the cases I have identified as reincarnation memories are not the result of ESP phenomena. Over the years I have found a good way to determine the difference. Reincarnation would seem to be the logical explanation if the person having the memories has not had any ESP experiences before or after the reincarnation memories and if that person has no conscious or unconscious knowledge of the area, history, period, or background of the material transmitted as reincarnation material.

DETAILS OF A "PLOT"

Consider the case of Pamela Wollenberg of Illinois, who was documented in the first chapter of my previous book, *Born Again*. Miss Wollenberg, a young hospital worker who never had been outside the United States and was not of Anglo-Saxon background, reported detailed, recurrent dreams pertaining to a Scottish political plot in the year 1600. She named names, gave dates, and described situations that I was able to later verify. Miss Wollenberg had had no ESP experiences prior to the recurrent dreams at age eighteen. She had no ESP experiences after the investigation was concluded. She had no access to the historical sources involved. Some of these sources were unpublished at the time of the investigation. After convincing myself that Miss Wollenberg was having reincarnation dreams, I broadened her ability to recall this alleged former life through hypnosis.

Hypnosis can assist in the probe of reincarnation memories, and there is often no reason not to attempt it. However, I do not believe it is productive to conduct reincarnation research exclusively through hypnosis. Rather, it should be used as a follow up when there is sufficient and substantial evidence of memories, recurrent dreams, or indications of unusual personality changes.

CONCLUSION

Hypnosis is an invaluable aid to investigation of the unexplained phenomenon of reincarnation. Clues that point to reincarnation include episodes of *déjà vu*, memories of a time and place about which the subject has no knowledge, and recurring dreams. Hypnosis facilitates regression, which can often verify the existence of a past life.

Conclusion

I have explained what hypnosis can, and cannot, do.

I have escorted you step by step through a hypnotic session and revealed the hypnotist's techniques.

I have separated modern hypnosis practiced by medical professionals from its occult-like past, as well as from the performance of stage hypnosis as entertainment.

I have warned, too, of the risks of self-hypnosis. Just as important, I have demonstrated how involuntary hypnosis takes place in public communications—advertising, publicity, and propaganda—that advances political and commercial messages, both positive and negative.

It is my hope that you will take from this book a more complete understanding that hypnosis, when administered professionally and under proper conditions, is a powerful tool that can help you face professional challenges, address personality issues, resolve problems of love, reject addictions, eliminate or reduce pain, and help resolve physical and mental problems. Remember, too, that these are just a few of the most common uses.

Hypnosis can also help individuals living with unexplained psychic phenomena seek answers, and is used extensively in research and investigation of parapsychology.

Not everyone can be hypnotized, and hypnosis doesn't help everyone. But it can help countless men and women find greater happiness and productivity while improving the quality of their lives.

Will you be one of them?

Glossary

Animal magnetism. A form of electric power with healing powers that eighteenth-century Swiss physician Friedrich Anton Mesmer, whom some have called the father of hypnotism, believed was channeled through the human body from an outer world.

Astral projection. A phenomenon in which a dreamer is said to propel from his or her physical body, traveling sometimes at high speed and great distances, while fully conscious of the journey. Also known as an "out-of-body experience."

Catalepsis. A state of rigidity induced by hypnotic suggestion, usually seen in stage hypnosis, in which the subject's body becomes so rigid that it can support great weights.

Conscious mind. The portion of the mind where logical thinking processes take place.

Déjà vu. An experience in which a person has a sudden, overwhelming sense of familiarity; translated literally as "already seen."

Dissociation of personality. A state induced under hypnosis in which the connection between the conscious and subconscious is temporarily loosened or severed.

Dream, symbolic. A dream with content that symbolizes the desires, objects, and problems of the dreamer.

Dream, true. A dream or series of dreams in which a person receives detailed, precise information about either past events unknown to the dreamer or future events, and which is remembered with clarity on awakening.

ESP. *See* Extrasensory perception.

Evil eye. In the Middle Ages, the evil eye, or so-called art of fascination, was a negative form of hypnosis in which a mere look from one person's eyes into another's was believed to result in a loss of will power in the recipient.

Extrasensory perception (ESP). The supposed ability of certain people to become aware of things by use of a perceptive sense beyond the five normal human senses; also known as the "sixth sense."

Guilt by association. Suspicion cast because of association with someone guilty or someone presumed to be guilty.

Hypnoanalysis. Conducting pyschoanalysis using hypnosis.

Hypnosis. A trance-like state in which the subject is more receptive to suggestions than in his or her ordinary state of consciousness.

Hypnosis, emotional. A term for hypnotic states induced by methods other than verbal commands, such as sound, motion, smell, and touch.

Hypnosis, involuntary. A form of hypnosis in which the unconscious mind is manipulated to form positive and negative preferences and opinions through forms of public communication such as advertising, publicity, and propaganda.

Hypnosis, silent. A form of hypnosis in which use of certain physical objects or telepathic commands may create a state of hypnosis.

Insomnia. Inability to sleep.

Medium. A person in a trance state whose speech and other functions are believed to be the communications of a foreign entity, thought to be a deceased person.

Occult. The sometimes secret practice of magic or witchcraft.

Out-of-body experience. *See* Astral projection.

Paranormal. Something unexplainable in the context of existing scientific knowledge.

Parapsychology. The study of unexplained psychic, or mental, phenomena.

Post-hypnotic suggestion. A command left by a hypnotist in the subconscious mind of a subject to be acted on later without the subject knowing the existence or source of the command.

Precognition. Knowledge of the future before it occurs.

Psyche. Human awareness in which the mind is the center of thought, emotion, and behavior; also known as the spirit or soul.

Psychic. A person possessing extrasensory perception (ESP).

Psychoanalysis. Therapy based on the theories of Sigmund Freud, whose work included dream interpretation and exploration of the unconscious mind in order to uncover and expose repressed impulses.

Psychology. Study of the human mind and human behavior.

Psychometry. A psychic ability to read past events where they occurred.

Psychotic. Schizophrenia, mania, and other mental disorders marked by delusions, hallucinations, incoherence, and jumbled perceptions of reality.

Rapid eye movement (REM). An index to the depth of a dream.

Regression. A process in which a person, under hypnosis, is gradually led back in time until the moment of birth is reached; in experiments related to reincarnation, regression is taken beyond the threshold of birth to supposed former lives.

Reincarnation. A phenomenon in which a person is believed to return to a new life in human form after one's death.

Schizophrenia. A form of mental illness generally characterized by delusions, hallucinations, and a loss of sense of reality.

Sixth sense. *See* Extrasensory perception (ESP).

Sleepwalking. A phenomena in which a dreamer's dramatic fantasy becomes so strong that it empowers the body to overcome the inertia of sleeping and to perform physical activity under direction of the unconscious mind.

Somnambulism. *See* Sleepwalking.

Soul. *See* Psyche.

Spirit. *See* Psyche.

Stage hypnosis. Hypnosis conducted for entertainment in front of an audience.

Symbolic dream. *See* Dream, symbolic.

Time slip. Phenomenon associated with reincarnation memories in which a person suddenly finds himself or herself in a different place and different time.

Trance state. A state of hypnosis in which a hypnotist can communicate with the subject's unconscious.

Transmigration. A belief that people, after death, are returned to new life in animal form.

True dream. *See* Dream, true.

Unconscious mind. A portion of the mind that does not perceive space or time, is unable to think logically, and through which feelings, emotions, and sometimes psychic experiences are channeled into the conscious mind.

Universal consciousness. A reservoir of information that is common to all people and is drawn upon by the unconscious mind.

World mind. *See* Universal consciousness.

Index

Religious ceremony, 83
REM. *See* Rapid eye movement.
Risks of hypnosis, 29–30
    inadequate time, 30
    injury, 30
    use of devices, 30–31
    use of substances, 31

S

Sedatives, 12, 31
Self-hypnosis, 34
Sexual intercourse, 15, 52
Shaman, 3–4
Sleep
    and hypnosis, 9–15
    importance of, 10–11, 15
    problems, 12–13
Sleep temples, 4
Sleep trance, 4
Sleepwalking, 12, 13–14, 16
Smells, 50
Somnambulism. *See* Sleepwalking.
Stevenson, Ian, 28, 90

Stewart, James, 74
Subliminal advertising, 56, 57
Suggestions in hypnosis, 35, 37–38,
    39, 40, 41, 42–43, 65, 67, 73

T

Telepathy, 81–82, 87
Time slip, 94–95
Touch, 51–52
Trance state, 28–29, 50
Transference, 26
Transmigration, 90

U

Unconscious mind, 9–10, 11, 12, 14,
    18, 25, 29
Universal consciousness, 10

V

Vicary, James, 56, 57
Visualizations, 39, 40, 41

W

Witches' cradle, 51

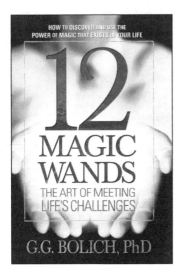

12 MAGIC WANDS

The Art of Meeting Life's Challenges

G.G. Bolich, PhD

Magic exists. It is everywhere. It surrounds us and infuses us. It holds the power to transform us. It isn't always easy to see, but then again, it wouldn't be magic if it was. Counselor and educator G.G. Bolich has written *Twelve Magic Wands*—a unique and insightful guide for recognizing the magic in our lives, and then using it to improve our physical, mental, and spiritual selves. It provides a step-by-step program that empowers the reader to meet and conquer life's consistent challenges.

The book begins by explaining what magic is and where it abides. It then offers twelve magic "wands" that can transform one's life for the better. Each wand provides practical tools and exercises to gain control over a specific area, such as friendship and love. Throughout the book, the author presents inspiring true stories of people who have used the magic in their lives to both help themselves and point the way to others.

The world can be a difficult place. Loneliness, disappointments, tragedies, and dead ends can sometimes seem insurmountable. Losing the magic in one's life can make it even more difficult. *Twelve Magic Wands* provides real ways to make it better—first inside, and then out.

About the Author

Dr. G.G. Bolich received his Master's of Divinity from George Fox University in Newberg, Oregon. He earned his first PhD in educational leadership from Gonzaga University in Spokane, Washington, and a second in psychology from The Union Institute in Cincinnati, Ohio. Currently a professor at Webster University in South Carolina, Dr. Bolich has taught courses at the university level since 1975. He also provides private counseling, specializing in trauma resolution, and is the published author of six titles and numerous articles in the fields of psychology, religion, and spirituality. Among his published works are *Psyche's Child, Introduction to Religion,* and *The Christian Scholar.*

$15.95 • 160 pages • 6 x 9-inch quality paperback • ISBN 0-7570-0086-X

OUR SECRET RULES
Why We Do the Things We Do
Jordan Weiss, MD

We all live our lives according to a set of rules that regulate our behaviors. Some rules are quite clear. These are conscious beliefs we hold dear. Others, however, are unconscious. These are our secret rules, and when we do things that go against them, we experience stress, anxiety, apprehension, and emotional exhaustion—and we never know why. That is, until now. In *Our Secret Rules,* Dr. Jordan Weiss offers a unique system that helps uncover our most secret rules.

The book begins by explaining the important roles that conscious and unconscious rules play in our daily existence. Each chapter focuses on a key area of our lives—money, religion, gender identification, work, friendships, health, power, personal expression, marriage, and sex. Within each chapter, there are challenging questions for the reader. The answers provide a personal look at how we are likely to behave when faced with specific situations. Each chapter ends with an analysis of potential answers that is designed to reveal the extent of our secret rules.

Our Secret Rules concludes by explaining how we can use our newly gained insights to improve the way we feel about ourselves and others. For once we are aware of our rules, we can then learn to live within their boundaries, or we can attempt to change them. And as we do, we can enjoy the benefits of happier, more harmonious lives.

About the Author

Dr. Jordan Weiss received his medical degree from the University of Illinois Medical School in Chicago. With an emphasis on the body-mind-spirit connection, he has worked at several leading complementary medical centers. A practicing psychiatrist for over twenty years, Dr. Weiss currently works at Irvine's Center for Psychoenergetic Therapy in California. He is the author of several published articles on emotional responses, and is a highly regarded speaker.

$12.95 • 184 pages • 6 x 9-inch quality paperback • ISBN 0-7570-0010-X

HOW TO **UNDERSTAND** AND **USE** THE **NUMBERS** IN YOUR LIFE

NUMEROLOGY
The Power in Numbers
Ruth A. Drayer

Numerology is the art and science of interpreting how numbers influence our lives and destinies. Over 2,000 years ago, Pythagoras, considered the first pure mathematician, felt that the key to understanding the universe was concealed in the science of numbers. By identifying and interpreting their hidden meaning and symbolism, he believed that we could gain insights into the past, present, and future. Today, numbers continue to hold a special place in our lives—birth dates, anniversaries, and, of course, our own personal "lucky" numbers. By studying our own unique set of numbers, we have within our grasp the tools to identify and examine the inherent and powerful forces that influence our lives and the lives of those around us.

Through the observation and understanding of your own unique numbers, you have the precious opportunity to gain greater insight into the nature of your personality— the shortcomings as well as the virtues—and create a blueprint by which you can live your life. Numerology provides the tools you need to reach that goal.

About the Author

Ruth A. Drayer has pursued the study of numerology for over thirty years, and has taught thousands of others her intuitive method of reading numbers. Through her private practice, she counsels clients from all over the world. A highly sought-after public speaker, Ms. Drayer has served as a facilitator at conferences and workshops on this subject throughout North America. She has also appeared as a guest-expert on numerous television and radio shows. A world traveler, artist, and mother of four, Ms. Drayer makes her home in southern New Mexico.

$15.95 • 192 pages • 6 x 9-inch quality paperback • ISBN 0-7570-0098-3

**For more information about our books,
visit our website at www.squareonepublishers.com**